to be
honest
with you

to be honest with you

A Journey of Certainty and Skepticism Through the Gospel of Luke

a book by
Vince Woltjer
and Tim Vandenberg

Authentic

Authentic Media
We welcome your comments and questions.
129 Mobilization Drive, Waynesboro, GA 30830 USA authentic@stl.org
and 9 Holdom Avenue, Bletchley, Milton Keynes, Bucks, MK1 1QR, UK
www.authenticbooks.com

If you would like a copy of our current catalog, contact us at:
1-8MORE-BOOKS
ordersusa@stl.org

To Be Honest With You
ISBN: 1-932805-08-7

Copyright © 2005 by Vincent Woltjer and Timothy Vandenberg

10 09 08 07 06 05 / 6 5 4 3 2 1
Published in 2005 by Authentic
All rights reserved. No part of this book may be reproduced in any form without permission in writing from the publisher, except in the case of brief quotations embodied in critical articles or reviews.

Scripture quotations marked CEV are taken from The Contemporary English Version. Copyright © 1995 by American Bible Society. Used by permission.

Scripture quotations marked NASB are taken from the NEW AMERICAN STANDARD BIBLE ®. Copyright © 1960, 1962, 1963, 1968, 1971, 1972, 1973, 1975, 1977, 1995 by The Lockman Foundation. Used by permission.

Scripture quotations marked NIV are taken from the HOLY BIBLE, NEW INTERNATIONAL VERSION ®. Copyright © 1973, 1978, 1984 by International Bible Society. Used by permission of Zondervan Publishing House. All rights reserved.

Scripture quotations marked NKJV™ are taken from the New King James Version®. Copyright © 1982 by Thomas Nelson, Inc. Used by permission. All rights reserved.

Scripture quotations marked NLT are taken from the *Holy Bible*, New Living Translation. Copyright © 1996. Used by permission of Tyndale House Publishers, Inc., Wheaton, Illinois 60189. All rights reserved.

Cover design: Paul Lewis
Interior design: Angela Duerksen
Editorial team: Michaela Dodd, Carol Pitts, Megan Kassebaum, Tom Richards

Printed in the United States of America

Contents

Introduction   vii

Luke 1
- 1–4   3
- 5–17   6
- 26–38   9
- 39–56   12

Luke 2
- 1–7   16
- 36–40   19

Luke 3
- 1–6   22
- 15–20   25

Luke 4
- 1–13   28
- 14–19   31
- 20–30   34
- 31–37   37

Luke 5
- 12–13   40
- 14–16   42
- 17–20   45
- 21–24   48
- 36–39   51

Luke 6
- 12–16   54
- 17–26   56
- 27–36   59

Luke 7
- 1–6   62
- 11–17   65
- 36–38   68
- 39–50   70

Luke 8
- 7–10   74
- 22–29   77
- 40–56   80

Luke 9
- 18–20   84
- 28–31   87
- 37–43   90
- 43–45   94
- 46–50   97
- 51–56   99

Luke 10
- 21–24   102
- 25–37   105
- 38–42   109

Luke 11		Luke 18	
1–13	112	1–8	161
14–28	115	23–30	164
33–36	119	35–43	167
Luke 12		Luke 19	
13–21	123	1–5	170
49–53	126	6–10	173
54–59	129		
		Luke 20	
Luke 13		9–19	175
1–9	132	27–40	178
18–21	135		
		Luke 21	
Luke 14		1–4	182
1–6	138	5–28	185
7–14	141		
		Luke 22	
Luke 15		14–22	189
1–2	144	23–30	192
3–10	146	39–46	195
		54–62	198
Luke 16			
1–9	149	Luke 23	
10–15	152	50–56	202
Luke 17		Luke 24	
3–10	155	9–12	205
11–19	158	13–32	207
		50–53	211

Introduction

This reflection on the Gospel of Luke began as a diary of my personal spiritual journey. A twenty-four-year-old student at the University of Michigan, I opened Luke's Gospel and read. As I read, I wrote about my world around me. I wrote about God's relentless pursuit of me, and Satan's effort to push me into despair. I wrote about my struggle to embrace my Redeemer, my fight for holiness, and my effort to answer the divine call to service. Over the next three years, I recorded my hopes, my fears, my anger, and my joy, the emotional suffering and spiritual yearning and intellectual searching of one young man. One day, I turned the page of my Bible to see I had reached the Gospel of John. I called my dear friend Tim and asked, "Will you help me take this stack of pages and make it worth sharing?" So Tim and I worked six more years, as he added his stories, insights, experiences, and spiritual hurdles. Until finally, the day arrived when it was time to release our work to others.

In the hope of being of service to God, we have opened our

souls for your observation. The title "To Be Honest With You" is in daily conversation a cliché, an introduction we use to tell others that we have something especially trustworthy to say. We pray that the pages to follow are painfully honest with you. We make public our weaknesses and our failings. We expose ourselves to possible criticism or even ridicule. But in the process, we pray that we reveal the expanse of Jesus' love and testify that our God is great. We regret only our unfulfilled wish to know you as well as you will know us. So please enjoy every last page. Maybe you will laugh. Or maybe you will read in silence. But no matter your pain or your doubt, please remember that Luke's Gospel brings you "good news of great joy that will be for all the people. Today in the town of David a Savior has been born to you; he is Christ the Lord."

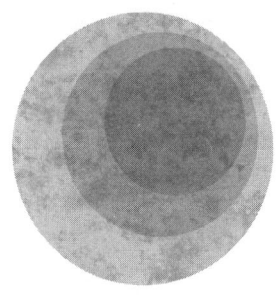

to be
honest
with you

Luke 1:1–4

> Many have undertaken to draw up an account of the things that have been fulfilled among us, just as they were handed down to us by those who from the first were eyewitnesses and servants of the word. Therefore, since I myself have carefully investigated everything from the beginning, it seemed good also to me to write an orderly account for you, most excellent Theophilus, so that you may know the certainty of the things you have been taught. {NIV}

I struggle to embrace with certainty the things I have been taught, the most important being things hoped for and things unseen. I flirt with doubt concerning the Christian faith and its invisible

God. My hands reach out to touch something—his nail-printed hands or wounded side—anything tangible to dispel the unmentionable nightmare of God as Fable. The existentialist taunts me that God as Myth dooms me to extinction, that God as Imaginary Friend robs me of innate value, and that God as Fairy Tale empties life of meaning. I have met the Angel of Death and Matthew the tax collector, but I want to see Jesus the risen shepherd, to feel his hand grip my own.

Fortunately, God shows me his footprints everywhere, left and right, forward and back, all over creation. Although Mark Twain asserts that "Faith is believing what you know ain't so," faith actually takes root in the soil of critical investigation. Creation itself invalidates theories of accidental origin and necessitates faith. As I compare empiricism to my parents' theistic faith, an all-powerful God points to the universe as his masterpiece, a puzzle too complex for self-genesis. I see a natural law that pays tribute to a designer and a world that begs to be recognized as art. The more grandiose the natural scheme, the more my doubting heart believes that this world must be a great handiwork.

In addition to the personal signature which God has stamped on creation, I have met God in my own experiences. For instance, the Holy Spirit replays in my mind memories of my grandfather's terminal illness, a window offering a view of God. I remember my grandfather, unhindered by fear of the unknown, eagerly awaiting the revelation of holy mysteries. As I reflect upon my grandfather's appointment with the Lord, I still hear the Holy Spirit's heavy footsteps pacing through my grandparents' home. These noisy footsteps drown out the derisive specter of uncertainty, as peace like a river calms my restless soul. A booming voice rather than a timid whisper shouts, "I AM," to all who will listen.

A doubt-free belief in God is a magnificent spiritual gift, one that I covet but do not possess, one that bestows unimaginable freedom to love and live. I recall one such belief-soaked friend who listened wide-eyed as I described my spiritual warfare against my empirical nature. She has never questioned whether she worships a God who lives in more than children's stories. I remember her sympathy for my uncertainty, her instinctive recognition that a Godless world would be a heartbreaking reflection of what could be permanently wonderful, but was instead fleeting and painful. Not possessing her gift, I doubt—but without embarrassment or jealousy. God has endowed me with only those gifts that he deems to be wise and appropriate. My uncertainty is not a moral failure, punishment from God, or a sign that he has discarded me. Rather, spiritual certainty is a privilege for which I will have to wait. The demons of my empirical nature shout with the cinematic Count of Monte Cristo that "I don't believe in God," but my soul and all of creation whisper back with the Count's priestly mentor, saying, "That doesn't matter, he believes in you."

Luke 1:5–17

It all begins with a Jewish priest, Zechariah, who lived when Herod was king of Judea. Zechariah was a member of the priestly order of Abijah. His wife, Elizabeth, was also from the priestly line of Aaron. Zechariah and Elizabeth were righteous in God's eyes, careful to obey all of the Lord's commandments and regulations. They had no children because Elizabeth was barren, and now they were both very old. One day Zechariah was serving God in the Temple, for his order was on duty that week. As was the custom of the priests, he was chosen by lot to enter the sanctuary and burn incense in the Lord's presence. While the incense was being burned, a great crowd stood outside, praying. Zechariah was in the sanctuary when an angel of the Lord appeared, standing to the right of the incense altar. Zechariah was overwhelmed with fear. But the angel said, "Don't be afraid, Zechariah! For God has heard your prayer, and your wife, Elizabeth, will bear you a son! And you are to name him John. You will have great joy and gladness, and many will rejoice with you at his birth, for he will be great in the eyes of the Lord. He must never touch wine or hard liquor, and he will be filled with the Holy Spirit, even before his birth. And he will persuade many Israelites to turn to the Lord their God. He will be a man with the spirit and power of Elijah, the prophet of old. He will precede the coming of the Lord, preparing the people for his arrival. He will turn the hearts of the fathers to their children, and he will change disobedient minds to accept godly wisdom." {NLT}

How often must Zechariah and Elizabeth have endeavored to understand why God had not entrusted them with children! In the deafening silence of an empty home, this couple must have longed to hear the pitter-patter of little feet. They may have taken excellent care of others' children, causing them to wonder why God had blessed them so stingily and so neglected their gifts. What an amazing discovery to learn that the Creator had spent decades seasoning them for their grand contribution.

I hear a gentle prelude as God smiles upon his good servants, Zechariah and Elizabeth. Melodic themes emerge as the Most High God sympathetically embraces the prayers of this elderly, barren couple. Each harmonious passage promises greater blessing to these prospective parents and to a waiting, downtrodden nation. In the magnificent finale, God's angelic courier pledges that this son will inherit Elijah's spirit as the Lord's messenger.

My God takes the stage as the grand mover and shaker, directing every instrument, weaving every note into a beautiful mosaic of sound. How reassuring to know that God tempers me for kingdom service through all events. Did my God not stretch out his hand to throw Jonah from his ship? Did my God not speak to stop Saul in his tracks? Does my God not number the birds of the air and clothe the lilies of the field? Although God may alter my dreams and test my patience, I as a dreamer, am no match for God as a schemer. I instead, like Zechariah and Elizabeth, listen carefully for the gentle song of my Father's call.

Luke 1:26–38

In the sixth month, God sent the angel Gabriel to Nazareth, a town in Galilee, to a virgin pledged to be married to a man named Joseph, a descendant of David. The virgin's name was Mary. The angel went to her and said, "Greetings, you who are highly favored! The Lord is with you." Mary was greatly troubled at his words and wondered what kind of greeting this might be. But the angel said to her, "Do not be afraid, Mary, you have found favor with God. You will be with child and give birth to a son, and you are to give him the name Jesus. He will be great and will be called the Son of the Most High. The Lord God will give him the throne of his father David, and he will reign over the house of Jacob forever; his kingdom will never end." "How will this be," Mary asked the angel, "since I am a virgin?" The angel answered, "The Holy Spirit will come upon you, and the power of the Most High will overshadow you. So the holy one to be born will be called the Son of God. Even Elizabeth your relative is going to have a child in her old age, and she who was said to be barren is in her sixth month. For nothing is impossible with God." "I am the Lord's servant," Mary answered. "May it be to me as you have said." Then the angel left her. {NIV}

In contrast to Zechariah's receipt of unbelievably good news, Mary received only unbelievable news. The angelic message signaled that the Almighty would tear away her social standing in God-fearing society and that providence would jeopardize her marriage to Joseph. Instead of wondering, "Who could believe such a story?" or "Who could accept such an offer?" Mary desired only to serve the Lord, requesting, "May it be to me as you have said." The angel then left Mary to deal with the consequences.

Educated in Donald Trump's television boardroom, I try to negotiate a better deal with God, one that brings fun, money, prestige, and the trappings of importance—one that recognizes that servanthood clashes with my positive self-image. I expect God to immortalize my features in stone as a lasting commemoration of my contribution. I toss and turn at night over the steep price, wondering if I can forsake my invitation to the *Headbanger's Ball* for the quiet sheep pen of Jesus. Worldly trinkets pull at my affections until Saint Francis of Assisi's prayer fades from my lips. My desire for earthly importance grips me as tightly as the precious ring of power enslaved Gollum. Slowly and subtly, Satan coaxes me to turn over the earring labeling me as God's slave.

Although I have forced my guardian angel to give more than one disappointing progress report to heaven, God nevertheless will not say, "You're fired." He insists that he will use me despite the dim reflection of Mary that I cast in the mirror. Memories of guilt wash over me—each selfish moment or flash of temper that has concealed the loving Christ. All suggest that I am of no use; but God does not let go. Discouragement threatens to launch me on another misguided quest for affirmation; but the Holy Spirit embraces this prodigal son and pries my fingers away from my earthly junk. Jesus' compassionate voice promises me a heart that thrills to take even the smallest place in the Kingdom of Heaven. I also am the Lord's servant.

Luke 1:39–56

A few days later Mary hurried to the hill country of Judea, to the town where Zechariah lived. She entered the house and greeted Elizabeth. At the sound of Mary's greeting, Elizabeth's child leaped within her, and Elizabeth was filled with the Holy Spirit. Elizabeth gave a glad cry and exclaimed to Mary, "You are blessed by God above all other women, and your child is blessed. What an honor this is, that the mother of my Lord should visit me! When you came in and greeted me, my baby jumped for joy the instant I heard your voice! You are blessed, because you believed that the Lord would do what he said." Mary responded, "Oh, how I praise the Lord. How I rejoice in God my Savior! For he took notice of his lowly servant girl, and now generation after generation will call me blessed. For he, the Mighty One, is holy, and he has done great things for me. His mercy goes on from generation to generation, to all who fear him. His mighty arm does tremendous things! How he scatters the proud and haughty ones! He has taken princes from their thrones and exalted the lowly. He has satisfied the hungry with good things and sent the rich away with empty hands. And how he has helped his servant Israel! He has not forgotten his promise to be merciful. For he promised our ancestors—Abraham and his children—to be merciful to them forever." Mary stayed with Elizabeth about three months and then went back to her own home. {NLT}

Summertime permitted us children to trade school drudgery for endless hours of baseball, neighborhood games, and swimming. Among the summer rites, even a mention of the trampoline invoked a reverent stillness. We loved the trampoline, the danger, the flips and spins. We breathed in freedom from white-man's disease every time we bounded off the sacred springs. Trampoline was not mere diversion, but a calling that demanded our blood and sweat as we perfected our Spiderman poses. One evening, as

I jumped in pitched battle with my arch-nemesis, Hobgoblin, my mother called me into the house. My mind raced for a reason why she had to permit me to jump late into the night on my beloved trampoline. Jabbing at the Achilles heal of her Baptist sentiments, I sprung to the rooftops and told her I could not obey because I was practicing for the rapture. I thought, "What premillennialist mother could terminate rapture practice?" Well, mine.

Speaking of rapture, I wonder if I alone pray to be "left behind"? The advantages of being left behind, both selfish and noble alike, seem so great. As one who struggles with uncertainty, I would welcome a front row seat to the miracle that I have so longed to see, in this case, my friends and family disappearing into the sky in marvelous testament to Jesus' triumph. Would not the sight of Ned Flanders bouncing into the clouds erase my doubt about whether Jesus has erased my guilt? More virtuously, I picture myself brawling through the last days of tribulation alongside Buck Williams, Buck Rogers and all the other famous Bucks. My heart aches for those without hope in Jesus, and I would rather submit to hard labor for their lost souls than take early retirement on the celestial beach. Would not my view of God's handiwork and the joy of my ongoing service far outweigh the disappointment of being left behind, for now? Heaven can wait, and my eternal wings can hang in God's closet. Just the sight of such a tribute to his victory would be enough to sustain me.

Elizabeth's leaping baby reminds me that Jesus has risen from the dead. As Mary says, the Mighty One has done great things. He remembers to be forever merciful, awarding a heavenly inheritance the day that Jesus buried my sin in hell, never to be seen or experienced or heard from again. So I bounce on my trampoline as I practice for a rapture I hope to avoid for a while. The springs strain and squeak as I reach for God. The fabric stretches as I invite others to join the fun. The earth disappears below as I tackle harder and riskier spiritual tasks. The wind whistles as I listen for the Lord's instruction. The sun warms my face as I bask in the Father's presence. One time, maybe, when the moment is right, I will not come back down.

Luke 2:1–7

At that time the Roman emperor, Augustus, decreed that a census should be taken throughout the Roman Empire. (This was the first census taken when Quirinius was governor of Syria.) All returned to their own towns to register for this census. And because Joseph was a descendant of King David, he had to go to Bethlehem in Judea, David's ancient home. He traveled there from the village of Nazareth in Galilee. He took with him Mary, his fiancée, who was obviously pregnant by this time.

And while they were there, the time came for her baby to be born. She gave birth to her first child, a son. She

> wrapped him snugly in strips of cloth and laid him in a manger, because there was no room for them in the village inn. {NLT}

I sometimes believe that I am alone in my discomfort with this Christmas card depiction of the infant Jesus. Although "Away in the Manger" and "Silent Night" dominate the Christmas carol Top 40, I would have preferred for Jesus to assume the more imposing image championed by movies. Movie heroes are rugged, iron-willed, handsome, intelligent, and invulnerable. While babies are awfully cute, I prefer to think of God as being more akin to Jack Ryan than the Gerber logo. But Jesus did *not* sweep down from the skies in a blaze of glory. He offered no catchy "I'll be back" or "You've been terminated" uttered from heaven with a heavy German accent. Instead, our first glimpse of the Son of the Most High God is a helpless baby—a special baby, to be sure—but an infant dependent upon parental care nevertheless. Jesus arrives as a child destined to carry the weight of the world's sin, not effortlessly or with cavalier pride, but oppressed by his burden.

This battered servant hardly conjures up the image that I want to emulate, making the Christmas story unsettling rather than quaint. I prefer Nietzsche's ideals and favor a proud persona, untouchable and larger than life. Could God not have come to earth with x-ray vision, a utility belt, web-shooters, and a conspicuous WWJD seal emblazoned upon his chest? Like the Zealots of Jesus' time, I would trade the providential plan for a more electric scheme. Without God's intervention, I would exchange humility for iron-willed toughness, not necessarily evil, perhaps, but less than useful unless subservient to Jesus' divine nature. If the Son of God can humble himself to assume the image of an infant, I can rearrange my priorities to pursue godly meekness rather than worldly pride.

Luke 2:36–40

Anna, a prophet, was also there in the Temple. She was the daughter of Phanuel, of the tribe of Asher, and was very old. She was a widow, for her husband had died when they had been married only seven years. She was now eighty-four years old. She never left the Temple but stayed there day and night, worshiping God with fasting and prayer. She came along just as Simeon was talking with Mary and Joseph, and she began praising God. She talked about Jesus to everyone who had been waiting for the promised King to come and deliver Jerusalem. When Jesus' parents had fulfilled all the requirements of the law of the Lord, they returned home to Nazareth in

> Galilee. There the child grew up healthy and strong. He was filled with wisdom beyond his years, and God placed his special favor upon him. {NLT}

The evangelical church risks serving a false god, an idol as wicked and seductive as ancient Baal. Humanism treads softly, quietly stealing the devotion we owe only to God. Some Evangelicals will protest and say that Christianity alone stands against secular humanism. Maybe, but it is a misdirected, even pious, humanism that covertly threatens our spiritual foundation. We say that salvation follows only when we take action to "believe in Jesus." In contrast to Abraham and Zechariah, who openly fought doubt, we at times equate faith with consistent belief, or worse yet, unwavering confidence. Pious humanism requires that salvation originate from my heart *within* rather than my Lord *without*. It replaces Jesus as Sacrificial Hero with Jesus as Invited Guest. While some claim to be co-agents of redemption, I renounce responsibility for ensuring that my feet trot through the pearly gates.

This kind of humanism that celebrates the belief of man over the sacrifice of Christ saps life from the evangelical community. We torment those endowed with a lesser gift of belief, suggesting inadequacy and implying insecurity regarding divine election. If uncertainty qualifies as sin, Jesus has made payment. When doubting Thomas sits nearby, we cannot steal his joyful inheritance by stating that uncertainty signifies a breakdown of providence or a breakup with God. In addition to personal pain, we suffer communally from unconfessed sin. We cannot admit to slighting God, by doubt or pride, because we cultivate an irrational fear of unbelief. How can we confess to doubt if it defrocks us as Christians? Nor can we request assurance if conviction is a prerequisite to legitimacy.

By way of contrast, Anna waited solely upon the Lord for deliverance and spoke only of his great deeds. Anna took no credit for God's favor but viewed everything through the prism of gratitude. In trusting God to save Jerusalem, Anna felt the suffering of divine focus but received the peace of divine responsibility. Anna's every word testified that God's mighty deeds over history guaranteed his mighty deeds in her heart. Anna prayed for others because she knew that God would not need her in order for the child to grow healthy and strong, to be filled with wisdom, and to be the recipient of God's favor.

God has kept in mind my humble, needy, and lost state. Willing to forgive even rebellion, as well as the lesser frailties of doubt, the Almighty offers peace before my knee shows the slightest bend. He extends mercy to a slow learner, endowing me not with unshakable conviction regarding his kingship, but devotion to his will in the midst of doubt and even anger. I doubt, but I confess no rock other than Jehovah. I waver, but I cling to no hope other than Jesus. I hesitate, but I embrace no master other than the Holy Spirit. So even in the darkest days of indecision, I will not despair that God has forsaken me, nor will a pious humanism convince me to replace petition with feigned confidence. Instead, I press on because faith is more a matter of the feet than the heart.

Luke 3:1–6

For fifteen years Emperor Tiberius had ruled that part of the world. Pontius Pilate was governor of Judea, and Herod was the ruler of Galilee. Herod's brother, Philip, was the ruler in the countries of Iturea and Trachonitis, and Lysanias was the ruler of Abilene. Annas and Caiaphas were the Jewish high priests. At that time God spoke to Zechariah's son John, who was living in the desert. So John went along the Jordan Valley, telling the people, "Turn back to God and be baptized! Then your sins will be forgiven." Isaiah the prophet wrote about John when he said, "In the desert someone is shouting, 'Get the road ready for the Lord! Make a straight path for him.

Fill up every valley and level every mountain and hill. Straighten the crooked paths and smooth out the rough roads. Then everyone will see the saving power of God.'" {CEV}

In high school, my friend Brett and I, in the spirit of Ferris Bueller, anticipated each visit by the United States Armed Forces. Displaying our desire "to be all that we could be," we volunteered to meet every visiting military recruiter, knowing that the United States would recommend to our school office that we, as prospective patriots, receive the coveted "excused absence." At the scheduled time, we listened to our uniformed guest's presentation and asked a few probing questions regarding helicopter maintenance. Brett would glance nervously at the clock before admitting to Uncle Sam that our less patriotic teacher expected our prompt return to class. I scanned the halls for bogies—teachers or hall-monitors—and we ran for the high ground called the mall. Fortunately, we were able to avoid the brig because teachers and military recruiters never paid attention to our actions or compared notes.

Unlike this *delinquentous* period in history, my acquaintances today *do* pay attention and *do* compare notes, judging the God to whom I publicly swear allegiance by the life that I privately live. In contrast to John's instruction that my words and deeds should proclaim the Lord's arrival, my tepid spiritual commitment and poor behavior tarnish the mirror image of Jesus that should appear each time I say hello. Gandhi said, "If it weren't for Christians, I'd be Christian." I fear that my acquaintance would have produced no change of heart for Mr. Gandhi. Who would really want to act like I act? Who would really want to meet my God because of me? My wrist displays a *What Would Jesus Do?* bracelet, but my actions suggest a *What Would Jezebel Do?* heart. It seems that I have much to do if my friends and neighbors are to "see the saving power of God" through me.

Although not the sharpest tool in the heavenly shed, I persevere in the assurance that the Holy Spirit will mold me into a useful servant. My imaginative God will transform me into one who straightens paths, fills valleys, and levels hills. He uses the weak, so I battle to serve knowing that from broken pieces, our God refashions instruments of his peace, both great and small.

Luke 3:15–20

The people were waiting expectantly and were all wondering in their hearts if John might possibly be the Christ. John answered them all, "I baptize you with water. But one more powerful than I will come, the thongs of whose sandals I am not worthy to untie. He will baptize you with the Holy Spirit and with fire. His winnowing fork is in his hand to clear his threshing floor and to gather the wheat into his barn, but he will burn up the chaff with unquenchable fire." And with many other words John exhorted the people and preached the good news to them. But when John rebuked Herod the tetrarch because of Herodias, his brother's wife, and all the other evil things he had done, Herod added this to them all: He locked John up in prison. {NIV}

While my heart cherishes grace, my pride suppresses a grateful sigh of relief that should accompany undeserved forgiveness and coaxes me to earn God's favor. My sin tugs at my shirt, suggesting that more good deeds will appease God's sense of justice. So I say my prayers of obligation, and I count my righteous acts, anything to hear my coins clang into the collection box for the purchase of indulgences. My pride drinks deeply of the works-righteousness elixir, and I reject the pangs of humility that inevitably accompany a plea for mercy.

The Bible introduces John, unlike heroes such as David or Peter, without mentioning a single character flaw. We know John only as obedient prophet, uncompromising martyr, and somehow unfit to tie Jesus' sandals. Setting aside Elijah's prophetic mantle for the redemptive Christ promised to Adam, John discards vain attempts to garner divine favor. John revels in grace, repudiating power in favor of messianic sacrifice, even in Herod's dungeon. A Gospel icon, John seizes the richness of submission and the blessing of a lesser state, squashing the crowd's sentiment that he might be the Christ. John, though nearly perfect, cannot wait to step aside in order to cast his lot with the Christ to whom he eagerly bows his head.

I would be wise to exchange my prideful independence for John's grateful subservience. In my actual weakness, Jesus necessarily serves as the protagonist in my biography, taking responsibility for securing my place with him. In light of John's admitted inadequacy to tie Jesus' sandals, should I presume to fasten the strings? I am no prophet, no Nazarene, no martyr, no maker of paths for messianic kings. I instead lay awake at night, imprisoned like Prometheus by my sin, suffering through memories of every unkind and wicked deed. If John needs the Lord, I need the Lord. If John steps aside, I should never even think to step up. As a first-class recalcitrant type, my Creative Memories book contains no montage of me opening the heavenly gate but only a single photograph of the Good Shepherd slinging my body, kicking and screaming, over his shoulder as he carries me home.

Luke 4:1–13

When Jesus returned from the Jordan River, the power of the Holy Spirit was with him, and the Spirit led him into the desert. For forty days Jesus was tested by the devil, and during that time he went without eating. When it was all over, he was hungry. The devil said to Jesus, "If you are God's Son, tell this stone to turn into bread." Jesus answered, "The Scriptures say, 'No one can live only on food.'" Then the devil led Jesus up to a high place and quickly showed him all the nations on earth. The devil said, "I will give all this power and glory to you. It has been given to me, and I can give it to anyone I want to. Just worship me, and you can have it all." Jesus answered, "The Scriptures say: 'Worship the Lord your God and serve only him!'" Finally, the devil took Jesus to Jerusalem and had him stand on top of the temple. The devil said, "If you are God's Son, jump off. The Scriptures say: 'God will tell his angels to take care of you. They will catch you in their arms, and you will not hurt your feet on the stones.'" Jesus answered, "The Scriptures also say, 'Don't try to test the Lord your God!'" After the devil had finished testing Jesus in every way possible, he left him for a while. {CEV}

For centuries, theologians and laymen alike have struggled with giving meaningful credentials to the satanic grand inquisitor. Both scholars and ordinary folk have expressed cynicism about whether Satan's offer could have enticed the Son of God. As Jesus prepares for events that will later cause bloody sweat to drip off his forehead onto the soils of Gethsemane, the serpent promises Jesus nourishment for his physical needs, dominion over all kingdoms, and respite from the terrible sinful burden he would later carry to the cross. Although never questioning Satan's power to fulfill his proposal, Jesus clings to God's will and refuses to yield to the benefits of satanic authority.

Temptation plagues my chronically weakened spiritual immune system. Notwithstanding my best effort to fight the good fight, both my personal sin and our communal sin testify to Satan's power. While I camouflage many of my failings from public view, my hidden disease is far deadlier than any open wound. Satan afflicts me with every attractive lie, referring often to a catalogue of my preferred temptations. I fall prey to those sins even though they ruin my prayer life. I leave the door open for the satanic ambassadors that depress me and detach me from God. Unlike David, I foolishly toss away my spiritual armor because it does not comfortably accommodate my evil companion. A pawn in spiritual warfare, I cannot imagine the crushing weight that Satan brought down upon a tired and hungry Jesus. Our Lord knows firsthand the depth of Satan's tempting power, that very influence that so quickly and completely overruns me.

More difficult to understand, I refuse to repudiate my friendship with sin. I pray earnestly, sometimes desperately, for God to remove my favorite sins from my life. However, even with the aid of prayer, I have not scrubbed my life clean with Jesus' blood. Nor do I remind Satan that Jesus has crushed his head, chained him, and terminated his dominion. I know that others, even people I admire as pillars of God's kingdom, struggle with a similar attachment to sin. While I have often heard speculation that the thorn Paul refers to was a physical handicap, I wonder if Paul's thorn was actually a deeply entrenched sin, a part of his former nature that he could not shake. I know neither the character of Paul's thorn nor why God does not remove my own, but I do understand that God has by his magnificent power freed me from slavery to Satan. Since God will use me for good despite my evil, I must persevere in faith, in hope, in prayer, and in a continuing expectation of freedom.

Luke 4:14–19

Then Jesus returned to Galilee, filled with the Holy Spirit's power. Soon he became well known throughout the surrounding country. He taught in their synagogues and was praised by everyone. When he came to the village of Nazareth, his boyhood home, he went as usual to the synagogue on the Sabbath and stood up to read the Scriptures. The scroll containing the messages of Isaiah the prophet was handed to him, and he unrolled the scroll to the place where it says: "The Spirit of the Lord is upon me, for he has appointed me to preach Good News to the poor. He has sent me to proclaim that captives will be released, that the blind will see, that the downtrodden will

be freed from their oppressors, and that the time of the Lord's favor has come."
{NLT}

In Mel Gibson's *Braveheart*, the cinematic portrayal of the Scottish revolution against the English crown, William Wallace, under torture, stuns the crowd by shouting out "Freedom!" rather than the cry "Mercy!" that would have ended his suffering but signaled his subservience. I marvel at his courage and his insistence upon liberty. God has created us in his own image, giving us autonomy, and a passion for freedom. Why else would Aleksandr Solzhenitsyn accept a dissident's exile? Why else would Martin Luther King Jr. march to Selma, Alabama? Why else would a lone student in Tiananmen Square stand before approaching Chinese tanks? God has created us with a desire for freedom coursing through our blood.

We do not become free by grasping for equality with God. The archangel Lucifer, who declared himself Jehovah's match, now lords over only a barren wasteland. Ancient man once built a Tower of Babel to reach heaven, but instead divided his community by geography and language. Friedrich Nietzsche has declared victory over a dead God, though he ended his life as a lunatic. Where today is the Thousand Year Reich or the communist utopia for those who would mock God as the people's opiate? Those who assert that God is inferior or irrelevant cannot free me.

In Jesus is the complete restoration of our freedom. If sin imprisons us, Jesus will release us into the glories of liberty. If we cannot see truth, Jesus will restore our sight. If we suffer oppression, Jesus will carry our burdens. He proclaims the year of the Lord's favor. I shout "Freedom!" because he frees me from that which the Heidelberg Catechism describes as "the tyranny of the devil." I no longer must cling to hate or live selfishly or submit to evil spirits of every imaginable shape and color. He instead casts away my sinful chains, empowers me to serve, and invites me to approach God with the boldest imaginable prayers. I can now draw close to my Lord, beg God for my neighbor's deliverance, and live each day in joy. "Free at last, free at last, thank God Almighty, we are free at last."

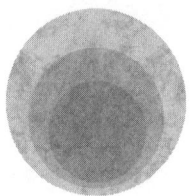

Luke 4:20–30

Jesus closed the book, then handed it back to the man in charge and sat down. Everyone in the meeting place looked straight at Jesus. Then Jesus said to them, "What you have just heard me read has come true today." All the people started talking about Jesus and were amazed at the wonderful things he said. They kept on asking, "Isn't he Joseph's son?" Jesus answered: "You will certainly want to tell me this saying, 'Doctor, first make yourself well.' You will tell me to do the same things here in my own hometown that you heard I did in Capernaum. But you can be sure that no prophets are liked by the people of their own hometown. Once during the time of Elijah there was no rain for three and a half years, and people everywhere were starving.

There were many widows in Israel, but Elijah was sent only to a widow in the town of Zarephath near the city of Sidon. During the time of the prophet Elisha, many men in Israel had leprosy. But no one was healed, except Naaman who lived in Syria." When the people in the meeting place heard Jesus say this, they became so angry that they got up and threw him out of town. They dragged him to the edge of the cliff on which the town was built, because they wanted to throw him down from there. But Jesus slipped through the crowd and got away. {CEV}

In many ways, Jesus resided in my hometown. My friends and I attended neighborhood churches, which were plentiful and outspoken. Local legend claimed that our McDonald's was the only one in the United States that Ronald closed on Sunday. Since God filtered my childhood through believing parents, a spirit-filled church, and a God-fearing community, Jesus walked beside me through my formative years. My environment made me a beneficiary of and obligated me to the Christian faith and lifestyle. There was, however, also the temptation to view our town as giving us special status with God.

Notwithstanding the spiritual silver-spoon upbringing, some

days I still march with the crowd that seeks to throw Jesus over the cliff. I share the crowd's spiritual interest, but I also live too close to Jesus to believe that my pedigree and hometown are not important to God. While they marvel at the miracle-working local boy made good, the Nazareth crowd sees Jesus only as Joseph's son, one who, as Messiah, should confirm their own importance as residents of Nazareth. They react angrily when instead Jesus says out loud that God has blessed Gentiles because he sees no special virtue in Israel, or Nazareth for that matter. I too watch the miracles, but relegate him to mere lifestyle choice or distant worldview, my eyes failing to focus on a savior calling to the repentant, not the entitled.

My vision blurs in an environment saturated with godly landmarks. The sign at the edge of town reads "Home of Jesus," giving me a false sense of importance rather than a need to change. I am so familiar with Clark Kent, that a meager set of glasses hides his identity as Superman. Familiarity does not breed contempt so much as indifference, as the apathy of affinity steals away the wonder and urgency of his message. We know Jesus not as the magnificent John Wayne but only as our own Marion Morrison, stripped of his mystique along with his stage name. It is unfortunate indeed, because the distinction of being the hometown prophet's neighbor, even if he is the Christ, means nothing to God.

Luke 4:31–37

He went down to Capernaum, a city of Galilee, and was teaching them on the Sabbaths. And they were astonished at His teaching, for His word was with authority. Now in the synagogue there was a man who had a spirit of an unclean demon. And he cried out with a loud voice, saying, "Let us alone! What have we to do with You, Jesus of Nazareth? Did You come to destroy us? I know who You are—the Holy One of God!" But Jesus rebuked him, saying, "Be quiet, and come out of him!" And when the demon had thrown him in their midst, it came out of him and did not hurt him. Then they were all amazed and spoke among themselves, saying, "What a word this is! For with

> authority and power He commands the unclean spirits, and they come out." And the report about Him went out into every place in the surrounding region.
> {NKJV}

My heart races when I consider the amazing grace that energizes the gospel. Jesus' status as Messiah endows him with authority. His message exudes power enveloped in a cloak of compassion. Both in Scripture and in life, God unleashes the gospel power to alter loved ones, sometimes beyond recognition. In Jesus' name, hardened criminals and hateful men, selfish and cold people, the apathetic and unwilling, all fall to their knees.

Even Son of Sam has learned that his crimes cannot place him beyond the reach of Son of God. I will never forget the video footage of the New York Police taking this demon-possessed serial killer into custody, with his evil, condescending, and hateful smirk. Nor will I ever forget, years later, this man's two hours of testimony on *Larry King Live*, during which he shared how Jesus had torn him free from Satan's grip. Secular psychiatrists and psychologists, of course, denigrate this marvelous transformation as the latest face of a delusional schizophrenic. However, even a casual observer of the redemption of David Berkowitz must wonder at the gospel power that has brought joy to such a dark heart and service to such formerly bloodstained hands.

The soul of David Berkowitz is a Holy Grail—a prize sparking spiritual warfare between the demon that instigated his horrible crimes and the Christ who paid for his marvelous redemption. Just like those who walked with Jesus in Galilee, I have, with Larry King's help, watched God cast demons from men.

Luke 5:12–13

Jesus came to a town where there was a man who had leprosy. When the man saw Jesus, he knelt down to the ground in front of Jesus and begged, "Lord, you have the power to make me well, if only you wanted to." Jesus put his hand on him and said, "I want to! Now you are well." {CEV}

In the great battle for men's hearts, Satan fears no image more than the compassionate Savior, mercy incarnate, touching the open wounds of the afflicted. If the Tower of Babel is to rise among the clouds, Satan must water down true empathy and blunt the spear of Christian compassion. So secularism offers popular alternatives to Christian mercy—sterile charitable activities that permit people to pretend they care in exchange for a minimal donation of money or time. Secular charity shields the public from personally meeting Jesus, an encounter that always occurs when one removes the sunglasses to see the suffering or peels off the latex gloves to touch the needy. We turn to the government or the United Way to excuse us from our responsibility to care, while also failing to introduce hurting souls to a merciful Lord. On the political right, we preach opportunity and responsibility, not God. On the left, we preach structural change and education, not God. Both sides throw money, whether as tax cuts or welfare, at people with needs that are truly spiritual in nature, making sure to stand far enough away to be safely unaffected. In public discourse, many verbalize compassionate thoughts, but only a few precious souls truly act compassionately. In simpler terms, Satan requires that bleeding hearts outnumber healing hands.

There is great hope for us sinners because Jesus compassionately healed the leper. In addition to merely "feeling our pain," Jesus bathes and binds our wounds. I must do the same for my neighbor whom Jesus loves. The outcast spirit, plagued by the sinful scourge, can expect a healing touch and rely upon a helping hand. Gospel power explodes when I touch the sick, deliver meals, tend to the aged, hand out blankets on a winter night, or serve as a mentor for children with a single parent. If a picture is truly worth a thousand words, then how beautiful is the image of Mother Theresa shuffling back and forth between the beds housing what the world considers to be Calcutta's garbage. I best understand compassion, along with its accompanying filth and ugliness, in the self-portrait that God painted for our viewing. Although cultural standards require him to grovel as unfit for human contact, the leper loves Jesus because the Lord touched his rotting skin.

Luke 5:14–16

Then Jesus ordered him, "Don't tell anyone, but go, show yourself to the priest and offer the sacrifices that Moses commanded for your cleansing, as a testimony to them." Yet the news about him spread all the more, so that crowds of people came to hear him, and to be healed of their sicknesses. But Jesus often withdrew to lonely places and prayed. {NIV}

In 1532, Francisco Pizarro, Spanish conqueror and governor of Peru, marched with two hundred men against the Inca Empire. At Cajamarca, Pizarro captured Chief Atahualpa, bragging of his conquests and stating that he had come to Peru that all might know God and his holy Catholic faith. Pizarro also held Atahualpa for ransom until the Inca had stacked enough gold objects to fill a room twenty-two feet long and seventeen feet wide. Despite a king's ransom, Pizarro sentenced Atahualpa to death. Francisco de Xerxes, Pizarro's secretary, described the scene:

> They brought out Atahualpa to execution; and, when he came into the square, he said he would become a Christian. The Governor was informed, and ordered him to be baptized. The ceremony was performed by the Very Reverend Father Friar Vicente de Valverde. The Governor then ordered that he should not be burned, but that he should be fastened to a pole in the open space and strangled. This was done, and the body was left until the morning of the next day, when the monks, and the Governor with the other Spaniards, conveyed it into the church, where it was interred with much solemnity, and with all the honors that could be shown it.

Atahualpa chose to strangle as a Christian rather than burn as a heathen. In such a fashion, Atahualpa, newest convert to Christianity, entered heaven literally at the hands of his Spanish missionaries.

While the church no longer advocates conversion at swordpoint, we still attempt to expand God's kingdom by threat and by force. Hellfire and brimstone rain down from our pulpits as the lost run for cover. We reduce eternal life—complete communion with God—to mere eternal fire insurance. When sharing Jesus, we threaten an ignominious end, rather than promise an indescribable beginning. When discussing God, we deliver painful tidings, rather than news too good to keep inside. Why do we fail to deliver on the Great Commission? We prefer a loud message to the Christ-like character that draws sinners to Jesus. Embracing the tactics of telemarketing, we talk more than we listen, and we badger people to buy our product. No threat—no matter how real or how vicious—can change my neighbor more than the Christian who, by listening, caring, helping, and encouraging, introduces my neighbor to the Jesus who loved so much that he carried sin into hell's deepest recesses.

In light of such grace, Jesus always interests me and overcomes diversion. If we watch our Lord, we observe that he often withdrew to lonely places to pray. Without the threats or shouts or hyperbole that we sometimes consider to be necessary to drive them to Jesus, we see that the crowds nevertheless surge towards him in search of physical healing, a few words of encouragement or wisdom, perhaps the hope of a glass of wine miraculously pressed from water, or simply the opportunity to sit in his presence. My job description includes no mention of saving souls, only the instruction to introduce others to the charismatic Christ. The Holy Spirit draws them to himself, not with fire or sword, not with threat of temporary hardship or eternal damnation, but with truth, unrestrained love, and a marvelous invitation whispered in a language of hope.

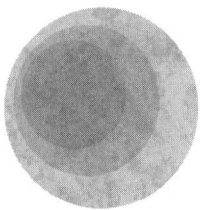

Luke 5:17–20

One day He was teaching; and there were some Pharisees and teachers of the law sitting there, who had come from every village of Galilee and Judea and from Jerusalem; and the power of the Lord was present for Him to perform healing. And some men were carrying on a bed a man who was paralyzed; and they were trying to bring him in and to set him down in front of Him. But not finding any way to bring him in because of the crowd, they went up on the roof and let him down through the tiles with his stretcher, into the middle of the crowd, in front of Jesus. Seeing their faith, He said, "Friend, your sins are forgiven you." {NASB}

It is said that it is good to have friends in high places. People pander to the rich and famous, whether for a favor or because such affiliations boost feelings of self-worth. Yet, one man with exaggerated western apparel and an affinity for twangy music, Garth Brooks, instead celebrates mates in low places. Friends of little earthly means or power, but very earthy character, also satisfy the need for companionship and affirmation. It appears that friends are valuable no matter where you find them.

Whether he had located them in high or low places, the paralytic man had terrific friends. These friends overcame tremendous obstacles to present their crippled companion to Jesus. While many so-called friends would have traveled only the easy mile, these friends dismantled a roof in order to lower their needy friend to Jesus' feet.

My friend, Wayne, and I were sixteen-year-olds when we attended a Christian youth convention. For days the sports, girls, entertaining speakers, and fun fully distracted me. We sat during stuffy summer days and pleasant evenings in the upper bleacher seats of the University of Rhode Island field house, listening to Dr. Anthony Campolo regale us with stories, entertain us with jokes, and reveal a stripped down gospel of Christian love and service. I laughed at every joke and hung on every story as I sweated away each day and lounged in the cool of each evening; but I miserably failed to transition from entertainment to transformation. I left each session chattering at Wayne about the great fun of this Rhode Island adventure. Eventually, my lack of perspective upset Wayne to the point of tears, a posture not altogether prudent for a sixteen-year-old boy, and he confronted me about my disinterest in spiritual matters. He dropped every semblance of teenage indifference and challenged me to see beyond that night's amusement to the Holy Spirit's message of eternal renovation. Wayne's disregard for ridicule dissipated my cloud of self-indulgence, and the following days changed my life.

These real friends understand you need Jesus, and they carry your mat if you cannot yourself walk. These friends set aside their comfort, risk their reputation, and subject themselves to hardship because they love you with Jesus' love. My friends like these are especially valuable because I can be a particularly heavy load to carry. With gratitude and admiration, I often consider what action I will take because every person should have a friend like Wayne.

Luke 5:21–24

> The Pharisees and the teachers of the law began thinking to themselves, "Who is this fellow who speaks blasphemy? Who can forgive sins but God alone?" Jesus knew what they were thinking and asked, "Why are you thinking these things in your hearts? Which is easier: to say, 'Your sins are forgiven,' or to say, 'Get up and walk'? But that you may know that the Son of Man has authority on earth to forgive sins. . . ." He said to the paralyzed man, "I tell you, get up, take your mat and go home." {NIV}

On a cold January night, I arrived at the gymnasium for a game in the church basketball league. The differential in the score rose and fell, tempers flared, perspective disappeared, and Christian fellowship deteriorated into a heated contest. As the game progressed, I relentlessly harassed the referee, taking advantage of his status as societal villain. I screamed, "Where is the foul?" He shrugged. I poked and chastised, wondering out loud why he had bothered to bring a whistle. He quietly reminded me that he would do his best as I exhausted my supply of complaints. That night, I lay awake wondering if I had been right about the calls—knowing that I had been wrong in my behavior. The next Sunday in church I was surprised by a tap on the shoulder from this same referee. He introduced himself with a smile and laughed when I apologized, instantly forgiving everything.

I wonder why Mike the Referee took a chance on me. The Torah teaches that it is hard to forgive sin. As my manners show, sinners bite. I think the merciful Christian resembles Steve Irwin, Australia's crocodile hunter, who searches the Australian outback for crocodiles and snakes to love—any creature that the public fears and avoids. Like Steve, the forgiving Christian jumps into the water, hanging on to the sinner for dear life despite all the "chomping and biting." In the end, the forgiving Christian excitedly praises the virtues of this marvelous creature, the sinner, exclaiming to the whole world that, "she's a beauty."

The church cannot be an exclusive club offering forgiveness as a perk available only to beautiful souls. We cannot be selective spiritual fishermen, passing on turtles and crocodiles and even some fish in search of a better catch. We cannot walk the stream, straining our eyes to find the trophy that would best decorate our beautiful church walls. I hope that no child will think that he or she should fish for men with a hook and a line rather than a net. Are we excited only when Ozzy and Harriet walk through our church door? Do we forget that Jesus was more likely to know a sinner, maybe Ozzy Osbourne, or a slave, say, Harriet Tubman? I love my church because it loves me, because sinners are not only welcome, but prized, and because it obeys the biblical mandate to be like Mike.

Luke 5:36–39

> Jesus then told them these sayings: No one uses a new piece of cloth to patch old clothes. The patch would shrink and make the hole even bigger. No one pours new wine into old wineskins. The new wine would swell and burst the old skins. Then the wine would be lost, and the skins would be ruined. New wine must be put only into new wineskins. No one wants new wine after drinking old wine. They say, "The old wine is better." {CEV}

During the muscle car movement of the 1970's (which lasted in my rural town well into the 1980's) my high school newspaper customarily ran a column called "Beater of the Month." This article invariably described in detail some student's heap of a car that the kid was "fixing up" into the hot-rod of his dreams. The picture depicted duct tape, jumper cables, an unattached muffler, and a stereo costing six months wages. Later, that same publication would print an *avant-garde* variation called "Cruiser of the Month," featuring a student vehicle that had been successfully "souped up" with a nice paint job, two fully attached mufflers, tinted windows, and a stereo that cost a full year's wages.

These newspaper articles, comfortable and familiar, have long been part of our community's tradition. They are old wineskins which, at their best, remind us of a lifestyle shaped by those wiser than ourselves. We can, as Christians, thank God for the precious traditions that anchor us to the infallible biblical revelation that the Christian band Petra so creatively called the "counsel of the holy." Customs crafted over centuries by judicious ancestors and grandparents are of great value, a reminder from experience of what really matters and should not be lightly set aside. In valuing our tradition, we should be mindful of the fact that God guided his church over centuries past just as we know he leads his church today. If even Jesus suggests that "the old wine is better," perhaps a prudent church preserves its old wine and presses new wine at a deliberate pace.

Some years later, at the school newspaper, my friend Brett and I wrote "Snow Sled of the Month," a tongue-in-cheek, human-interest piece about a friend and his remodeled sled. We followed our debut with "Employee of the Month," a satirical profile of a school candy shop worker. My journalistic career peaked with "Headbanger of the Month," a probing exposé on a classmate with big hair and the motto "If it's too loud, you're too old." Students laughed and teachers smiled, but some parents disapproved of any suggestion that "Beater of the Month" was no longer relevant as well as any mention of a "Devil's Music" culture different from their own. So ended "Headbanger of the Month," a departure from "Beater of the Month" too far ahead of its time.

As Brett and I learned from our disappointing Geraldo imitation, we cannot as Christians stand on tradition to the point of irrelevance. At its worst, tradition can elevate habit to the status of a golden calf, an idol compelling us to act as we have always acted no matter the shape of the worldly challenge that God calls us to confront. Jesus tells us that new wine—in our case a society changing in form—requires new wineskins, namely a change in our traditions. *The Godfather* contains a scene in which the family's violent crucifix-adorned henchmen stand around the baptismal font before whacking another soul. For these fictional characters, the baptismal font represents only empty tradition, an old wineskin cracked by violence and drained of the obedience to God that baptism formerly signified. If our biblical mandate is to remain vibrant and visible, we need new wineskins to hold the new wine that pours forth when each new generation interacts with its world.

Jesus must shake his head at both the revolutionary who will not respect tradition and the reactionary who worships it. Yet, our churches split over such issues because it is so hard to differentiate between that which we have always done and that which we must always do. Our only response can be prayer. Lord, equip us to engage our world and keep us from spilling even one drop of new wine. Lord, preserve us and keep us from spoiling the old wineskins that our forefathers passed down.

Luke 6:12–16

> Now it came to pass in those days that He went out to the mountain to pray, and continued all night in prayer to God. And when it was day, He called His disciples to Himself; and from them He chose twelve whom He also named apostles: Simon, whom He also named Peter, and Andrew his brother; James and John; Philip and Bartholomew; Matthew and Thomas; James the son of Alphaeus, and Simon called the Zealot; Judas the son of James, and Judas Iscariot who also became a traitor. {NKJV}

A motley crew of former fishermen, tax collectors, and others of little note, the disciples were selected for unknown reasons. These twelve made mistakes, misunderstood their lessons, and squabbled. They likewise sacrificed family, occupation, and security to follow Jesus. In spite of their mixed legacy, the Holy Spirit transformed these commonplace Peter Parkers into great figures. God again engraved the portraits of ordinary people onto the mural of history, complementing his choice of a man with stage fright to challenge a Pharaoh, a bodybuilder with bad taste in women to fend off Philistia, and an adolescent harpist to slay a giant.

In elementary school, my best friend was our finest athlete. Being first-team, all-conference in dodge ball, he carried us to new heights of gym-class glory in this game of skill, strategy, and perseverance. The education gods smiled as smaller kids ran for the corners with their arms covering their heads. One day, however, my friend failed to pick me for his team, instead choosing a less-talented buddy of the plumper variety. Despite my absence, my friend's team of the average prevailed as he carried them to victory. When I confronted my buddy about the injustice he had inflicted upon me, he refused to repent, justifying his decision as necessary to give this plumper companion the chance to participate in great deeds.

God performs great works through run-of-the-mill people. Gospel power stems not from a minister's elegant words, ornate buildings, or organized political-action committees, but from God empowering willing servants to act selflessly. Consistent with his historical intervention, the Holy Spirit pushes ordinary people to greatness. It matters little what I bring to the table because anybody can serve, anybody can love, and anybody can share Jesus with another. When the Spirit flows through me, I experience "Holiday Inn Express syndrome." I, like the apostles, do things beyond my capabilities because I am well-rested in the Lord.

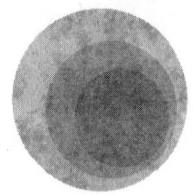

Luke 6:17–26

He went down with them and stood on a level place. A large crowd of his disciples was there and a great number of people from all over Judea, from Jerusalem, and from the coast of Tyre and Sidon, who had come to hear him and to be healed of their diseases. Those troubled by evil spirits were cured, and the people all tried to touch him, because power was coming from him and healing them all. Looking at his disciples, he said: "Blessed are you who are poor for yours is the kingdom of God. Blessed are you who hunger now, for you will be satisfied. Blessed are you who weep now, for you will laugh. Blessed are you when men hate you, when they exclude you and insult you and reject your name as evil, because of the Son of Man. Rejoice in that day and leap for joy, because great is your reward in heaven. For that is how their fathers treated the prophets. But woe to you who are rich, for you have already received your comfort. Woe to you who are well fed now, for you will go hungry. Woe to you who laugh now, for you will mourn and weep. Woe to you when all men speak well of you, for that is how their fathers treated the false prophets. {NIV}

The saga of Frasier Crane, my all-time favorite television character, ended. For eleven years, I had marveled at the ingenious scripts and wondrous talent of Kelsey Grammer and David Hyde Pierce. In the final episode, the writers of this comedic masterpiece offered a parting gift to each primary character. To Niles Crane and Daphne Moon, the writers left a son, a symbol of new life. To Roz Doyle, the writers conferred a promotion to KACL station manager, a means to prosperity. To Martin Crane, the writers presented a wife, Ronee Lawrence, a companion. To Dr. Frasier Winslow Crane, the writers gave a new city and a new love, in essence, a fresh start. As Frasier's airplane landed in Chicago, I turned off the television knowing that life would offer Frasier Crane happiness and opportunity.

Jesus promises his followers consequences that often appear at first blush to be not nearly so attractive as the collection of prizes given to the entourage of Frasier Crane. Taking advantage of this reality, Satan turns his earthly kaleidoscope to mesmerize me with material ornaments and worldly opportunity, all available for the right price. A search for riches forbids generosity. A bountiful table conceals the reality that God alone fulfills need. A veneer to cover suffering, laughter can smother the calls of the oppressed. Man's approval reduces God's endorsement to secondary importance. Satan whispers that Christianity's only reward is its remarkable retirement plan.

Jesus startles me to my senses, and I scurry to reestablish my priorities. I race to accept the "gifts" described by Jesus like a man holding a winning lottery ticket. When I hunger for God, I speak constantly to him. When my heart becomes poor, I stand firm against the mirage of temporal happiness. When I weep, Christ's compassion flows through my soul and my hands, making me discontent with misery and intolerant of injustice. When my peers ridicule me, I know my Christianity to be sufficiently visible as to be offensive to those who oppose God. It is a strange set of blessings, those being poverty, hardship, tears, and insult; but they are blessings indeed because they unmistakably signify a Spirit-filled disciple walking the narrow path of obedience.

Luke 6:27–36

But if you are willing to listen, I say, love your enemies. Do good to those who hate you. Pray for the happiness of those who curse you. Pray for those who hurt you. If someone slaps you on one cheek, turn the other cheek. If someone demands your coat, offer your shirt also. Give what you have to anyone who asks you for it; and when things are taken away from you, don't try to get them back. Do for others as you would like them to do for you. Do you think you deserve credit merely for loving those who love you? Even the sinners do that! And if you do good only to those who do good to you, is that so wonderful? Even sinners do that much! And if you lend money only to those who can repay you, what good is that? Even sinners will lend to their own kind

> for a full return. Love your enemies! Do good to them! Lend to them! And don't be concerned that they might not repay. Then your reward from heaven will be very great, and you will truly be acting as children of the Most High, for he is kind to the unthankful and to those who are wicked. You must be compassionate, just as your Father is compassionate. {NLT}

Although we all acknowledge knowing disagreeable souls with whom we struggle to peacefully coexist, sometimes we secretly guard a blacklist of enemies deep in the heart's dungeon. We lie awake at night staring into the hazy crystal ball of memory, recounting offenses, both trivial and stunningly hurtful, that stoke fires of hate. Our thoughts skip past those merely disliked to those truly reviled, as adrenaline clenches fists and grits teeth. The tears flow, the stomach churns, and vitriolic curses pass almost silently over the lips. The detested have often earned their disdain, but occasionally our resentment results from bias or imagination. All the abhorred become enemies in a frighteningly seamless transition.

Where the fruits of the Spirit shrivel and the weeds of hate bloom, we find the dreadful grub, pride, chewing away the humble roots that anchor us to God. We understand pride's destructive power, but we refuse to release unjustified animosity or rightful vengeance. Men show open hostility to each other, untroubled by the knowledge that disobedience is the price of posturing. Women smile and laugh together, yet each is ready to bury the knife in her neighbor's back the moment a head turns. For both genders, periods of remorse can be few and far between. Our wounded pride paces the soul's prison without shackles, smashing any seedling of forgiveness that sprouts in the cracks of the hardened heart.

We have cheaply sold our precious peace for petty pride. Like Esau, we have traded our God-given birthright for Goldilocks' leftovers. In place of the redeemed sinner's indescribable joy, we substitute the hellish quest for vindication. We chase after the one who hurt us, rogue or thief, all the while evading the God to whom we owe payment for a great crime. Will hate heal the heart? Will retaliation reverse the wrongdoing? Will bitterness salve the wounds? My hate smothers my delight in the Lord and my service to his Church while being strangely inadequate to satisfy my pride's appetite.

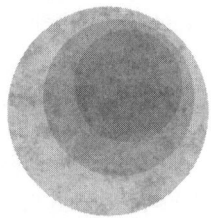

Luke 7:1–6

Now when He concluded all His sayings in the hearing of the people, He entered Capernaum. And a certain centurion's servant, who was dear to him, was sick and ready to die. So when he heard about Jesus, he sent elders of the Jews to Him, pleading with Him to come and heal his servant. And when they came to Jesus, they begged Him earnestly, saying that the one for whom He should do this was deserving, "for he loves our nation, and has built us a synagogue." Then Jesus went with them. {NKJV}

I know godly people, each with faith greater than the symbolic mustard seed, who have not received from God that for which they have asked. I remember my grandparents' faith, but my grandfather died from cancer and my grandmother lives alone. I watch parents pray for children, but they still wait for grace. I see lives crippled by disease or overrun by all manner of trouble. None of us wish for these trials. These hearts, each as deserving as the centurion, if one can deserve grace, all cry out for Jesus' healing touch.

While I have heard stories of miraculous healing credited to a believer's faith, I cringe when some suggest that healing is the shadow that follows faith. Two individuals grasp Jesus' fingers, yet only one lifts thankful hands to heaven while the other continues to groan in pain. Have we not all held a loved one who longs for death's numbing touch? I wonder if God is arbitrary in distributing his healing grace.

Fyodor Dostoyevsky has perfectly painted this picture in the compelling *Brothers Karamazov*. Ivan Karamazov cannot accept a God who permits the suffering of innocent children, stating that he chooses to "return him the ticket" to eternal life. More recently, I have watched Buffy the Vampire Slayer refuse immortality because the price included innocent suffering. *The Gulag Archipelago*, *Schindler's List*, *The Killing Fields*, and the abortion video, *Silent Scream*, make it hard to believe that "all things work together for good to those that love God and are called according to his purpose." I will not agree that the greater good justifies a suffering innocent, but only a Suffering Innocent has secured my salvation.

Only by turning to God can I reconcile the dilemma of a compassionate Savior and suffering. God does not bestow limitless compassion at one moment and curses the next. Creation testifies to God's power and history refutes the contention that God is ambivalent. So I ask, why? The answer, dissatisfying as it may be at times, is that God's kindhearted plan is more complex than I can understand with my earthly limitations. Experience teaches me to view events within the context of daily life. I find it hard to grasp a plan that begins before my existence and extends beyond my death. He restores us later than I would have hoped and differently than I would have expected. True faith—action based upon observation, critical thought, and biblical promise—constitutes my only sane response. God does not permit suffering due to ambivalence or powerlessness. Faith is the only foothold when bad things happen to good people.

Luke 7:11–17

Soon afterward Jesus went with his disciples to the village of Nain, with a great crowd following him. A funeral procession was coming out as he approached the village gate. The boy who had died was the only son of a widow, and many mourners from the village were with her. When the Lord saw her, his heart overflowed with compassion. "Don't cry!" he said. Then he walked over to the coffin and touched it, and the bearers stopped. "Young man," he said, "get up." Then the dead boy sat up and began to talk to those around him! And Jesus gave him back to his mother. Great fear swept the crowd, and they praised God, saying, "A mighty prophet has risen among us," and "We have seen the hand of God at work today." The report of what Jesus had done that day spread all over Judea and even out across its borders. {NLT}

We have all watched another lay a loved one to rest. In circumstances this inherently tragic, our hearts sink, our eyes blur with tears, our hands tremble, and our voices fail us. We remember our own experiences with heartbreak and grieve for people in their sorrow. Death humbles me since I am invariably powerless to replace that which was lost. Empathy is wholly spiritual because only God can offer comfort. Christian compassion is communal because each of us can generate intense love for another.

Death derives its tremendous importance from its inevitability, unpredictability, and brute force. The term *death* connotes coldness, emptiness, and a grave finality. Our culture fixates upon death as our artistic icons try to convince us that we can triumph over the Angel of Death through battle or laughter.

I remember the news coverage of Jerry Garcia's death. The media has glorified Jerry as a man who cheated death through years of substance abuse and who joked about death until the end. But death has finally defeated Jerry, and while I am unsure whether Jerry is grateful, I know that he is dead. Jerry is foolish for treating so lightly such a weighty event. In his exchange of jokes with Jerry, the Grim Reaper has had the last laugh.

The widow's story restores my hope because I see that Jesus

suffers with each person who feels death's sting. In his humanness, he sets aside heavenly splendor to assume our weakness against our impending demise. As God's son, he reclaims people to life even from the grave. Neither special nor unique, the widow, like us, receives divine reprieve, a sign that authenticates Jesus as Messiah and a miracle that declares him Lord over even sin's darkest consequence. While one can wonder at Jesus' special outpouring of peace, we take comfort because he has only foreshadowed his greater work. Death's pain would be unimaginable without the promise of life from the Christ's comforting hand. Revealing mastery even over death, God has indeed come to help his people.

Luke 7:36–38

> Then one of the Pharisees asked Him to eat with him. And He went to the Pharisee's house, and sat down to eat. And behold, a woman in the city who was a sinner, when she knew that Jesus sat at the table in the Pharisee's house, brought an alabaster flask of fragrant oil, and stood at His feet behind Him weeping; and she began to wash His feet with her tears, and wiped them with the hair of her head; and she kissed His feet and anointed them with the fragrant oil. {NKJV}

As the warm fall breezes pranced through the rainbow foliage forming a canopy over Cedarville College, my friend Ron escaped from his dormitory on his daily walk to class. Ron's spirits, already sky high from a gorgeous sunny day, picked up as his ever-vigilant senses detected the approach of a girl of extraordinary personal interest. His heart raced faster as he debated whether to feign cool indifference or risk everything by saying hello. In a moment of extreme courage, Ron delivered a wink and a snappy greeting, observing the unmistakable flash of a smile from her lips. Ron floated to class, his posture straightened and his thoughts awash with possibilities. How could he have doubted himself? He should have known that she could not resist his Ron-tastic charms. He turned to view his reflection in a nearby window only to discover that he had made his move with his zipper down and his shirttail prominently displayed where his jeans should have been. That smile, though gracious and kind, owed no allegiance to either her admiration or his personal magnetism. At that moment, Ron really knew grief.

    I thank God that he has taught me to really grieve over my sin. When I was younger, I would struggle to feel sorry for my transgressions. I would feel bad when I did wrong if I got caught, but my heart never broke over turning my back upon God. Unlike the repentant woman, perhaps renowned for her sin, my tears would not fall, I would not hang my head in shame, nor would I pour out my gratitude at the master's feet. My best moments with God now come when I recognize my need for forgiveness and fully, publicly, and unconditionally call out to Jesus. I now depend wholly upon his grace; my faith has matured. Perhaps my sins have intensified; nevertheless, he lifts my burden. At these times I understand gratitude. I usually swear that I will not sin again, a promise I never keep. But the Lord restores my soul to its intended usefulness and beauty. I breathe easier knowing that I need not rely upon my Tim-tastic charms.

Luke 7:39–50

When the Pharisee who had invited him saw this, he said to himself, "If this man were a prophet, he would know who is touching him and what kind of woman she is—that she is a sinner." Jesus answered him, "Simon, I have something to tell you." "Tell me, teacher," he said. "Two men owed money to a certain moneylender. One owed him five hundred denarii, and the other fifty. Neither of them had the money to pay him back, so he canceled the debts of both. Now which of them will love him more?" Simon replied, "I suppose the one who had the bigger debt canceled." "You have judged correctly," Jesus said. Then he turned toward the woman and said to Simon,

"Do you see this woman? I came into your house. You did not give me any water for my feet, but she wet my feet with her tears and wiped them with her hair. You did not give me a kiss, but this woman, from the time I entered, has not stopped kissing my feet. You did not put oil on my head, but she has poured perfume on my feet. Therefore, I tell you, her many sins have been forgiven—for she loved much. But he who has been forgiven little loves little." Then Jesus said to her, "Your sins are forgiven." The other guests began to say among themselves, "Who is this who even forgives sins?" Jesus said to the woman, "Your faith has saved you; go in peace." {NIV}

Like the sinful woman, I wonder that God imposes no limit, either quantitative or qualitative, on forgiveness. I slowly exhale as I consider both the great expanse and expense of my sin. I have reduced my collection of public sins, and others see me as a decent citizen, but God may have a different view. Apathy about sin—in light of forgiveness bestowed by grace—may offend God more than bad deeds performed in ignorance. Yet, Jesus spends no time calculating sin quotients, concerning himself instead with repentant hearts rather than worthy souls. It is no surprise that the sinful woman continued anointing the Savior with oil and kissing his feet.

Notwithstanding forgiveness, sin remains serious business. I must confess that as a teenager I nearly shot my dad while fooling around on a deer-hunting trip. I occasionally shake awake from a nightmare about these events. If I had shot my dad, forgiveness would not have spared my mother from loneliness at my hands. Or consider one who dismantles the virtuous defenses of a young woman with the tools of manipulation, lies about love, and false promises of marriage. The Lord may forgive the perpetrator, but his selfishness still scars an expectant bride. So can we quickly forgive ourselves knowing that only the death of David the king delivered David the father from the pain of Absalom's betrayal? Jesus' blood may be more effectual than the water in Lady Macbeth's basin, but I delude myself if I tritely declare forgiveness and walk away without the slightest pang of guilt about the plundered villages that lie at my feet.

So Christian, play your part in Daniel DeFoe's great novel *Robinson Crusoe*. In this harrowing tale of adventure and redemption, Robinson Crusoe rescues a doomed man, renamed Friday, from certain death at the hands of headhunters. Friday's gratitude to his redeemer compels him, despite hardship, trepidation, and journey, to faithfully serve Crusoe for life. The forgiven sinner must also answer to the name Friday. We must joyfully embrace our freedom from the doom of sin. Like the sinful woman, we must greatly love the Lord. Yet, we take on more than Friday's smile, the joy that accompanies deliverance from destruction. We must also welcome slavery to a benevolent master who demands repentance. I too, like the sinful woman, shall cover Jesus' feet with my tears because I am truly sorry. The forgiven do not forget their shame. The forgiven do not forget their debt. So call me Friday, for I am grateful. Call me Friday, for I can smile. Call me Friday, for I am alive and well.

Luke 8:7–10

"Other seed fell among thorns, which grew up with it and choked the plants. Still other seed fell on good soil. It came up and yielded a crop, a hundred times more than was sown." When he said this, he called out, "He who has ears to hear, let him hear." His disciples asked him what this parable meant. He said, "The knowledge of the secrets of the kingdom of God has been given to you, but to others I speak in parables, so that, "'though seeing, they may not see; though hearing, they may not understand.'" {NIV}

Although I cannot comprehend him on my own, God reveals himself, his creation, and his wondrous salvation. Jesus rejects the role of cosmic dungeon master, and the Bible contains neither Yoda's riddles nor Calgon's ancient Chinese secrets. The Discovery Channel, in *Mysteries of the Bible*, wrongly claims that God obscures truth like parents who spell out C-A-N-D-Y in their clandestine language. The Bible describes three simple truths. First, I am a sinner deserving eternal separation from God. Second, God loves me so dearly that he sent Jesus to pay for my sin. Third, my gratitude to God for this free gift compels me to treat people as Jesus would treat them. Everything else adds flavor and depth but does not change the story.

Jesus' parable teaches us that a wise person understands God's revelation only through action. Although I can easily *see* God's message, I must complete the more difficult and very Jewish task of seeing by acting. Although I can easily *hear* God's message, I must complete the more difficult and very Jewish task of hearing by obeying. The Beatles, not God, have coined the phrase "All you need is love," as if emotion satisfies the demand for action. The book of James shatters that illusion, reminding us that faith without deeds is dead—not second-rate, not unrealized potential, not even inadequate, but dead.

Jesus' parables are not so much confusing as expensive to implement. Believers of all ages and talent levels hear the Lord's call. God's Word is not elitist, confusing, or inaccessible. The Holy Spirit is universally understandable and approachable. For example, while the Lord gives us nets, some refuse to fish. A large harvest would require so much hard work and sacrifice. I know the benefit of spiritual exercise, but television offers an enjoyable distraction and walking hurts my feet. So I call out, "Oh Lord, please show me your will for my life," in the same way I used to tell my mother that I could not hear her call me for dinner when I wanted to play outside. While some may indulge in the excuse of holy perplexity, I must transition from spectator to participant.

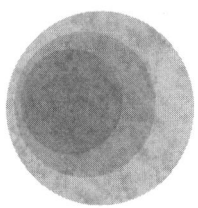

Luke 8:22-29

One day Jesus said to his disciples, "Let's go over to the other side of the lake." So they got into a boat and set out. As they sailed, he fell asleep. A squall came down on the lake, so that the boat was being swamped, and they were in great danger. The disciples went and woke him, saying, "Master, Master, we're going to drown!" He got up and rebuked the wind and the raging waters; the storm subsided, and all was calm. "Where is your faith?" he asked his disciples. In fear and amazement they asked one another, "Who is this? He commands even the winds and the water, and they obey him." They sailed to the region of the Gerasenes which is across the lake from Galilee. When Jesus stepped ashore, he was met by a demon-possessed man from the town. For a long time this man had not worn clothes or lived in a house, but had lived in the tombs. When he saw Jesus, he cried out and fell at his feet, shouting at the top of his voice, "What do you want with me, Jesus, Son of the Most High God? I beg you, don't torture me!" For Jesus had commanded the evil spirit to come out of the man. Many times it had seized him, and though he was chained hand and foot and kept under guard, he had broken his chains and had been driven by the demon into solitary places. {NIV}

My teachers at church have at times incompletely described Jesus' true identity. These role models know Jesus as God, but they have been so dedicated to explaining Christ's love that they have overemphasized Jesus as friend. While the old hymn "What a Friend We Have in Jesus" roots itself in solid theological ground, we rarely see new songs dedicated to God's power or his demand for justice. Our reverent hymnbook, full of awe-inspiring and sometimes frightening hymns, has evolved into a sensitive projector overlay, with choruses that rightfully claim that God loves but rarely remind us that God commands. My mighty fortress has become my pen-pal from summer camp, a comrade in games, and a sympathetic ear in which to pour out the pain of homesickness but not my rock and my Lord. While God created me for worship and relationship, do we worship God Almighty, or have we instead given our hearts to Tickle Me Jesus?

My secular education also instills error about Jesus' true identity. In pampered America, we have assigned Jesus the position of Santa's little brother, a type of Chief Elf. While they may together keep a list of who is nice and who is behaviorally challenged, Santa and Jesus will in the end give gifts to children of all cultures and religions. Both Santa and Jesus know to stay in their respective domains, one at the mall and the other at church. We may admit that Jesus is more authentic than Santa, but only if he respects the safe confines of divine irrelevance, keeping out of the public square, the school, the research laboratory, the home or anywhere else where people make important decisions.

By way of contrast, the biblical Jesus exercises power beyond imagination. Jesus stops wind from blowing and storms from raging. Demons powerful enough to drive men insane beg for mercy in his presence. As creator, Jesus exercises lordship over all, commands forces beyond understanding, and speaks with God's authority. Jesus loves me intensely, and he has suffered greatly to spare me from the abyss. As God's adopted child, I walk fearlessly into his presence, but never without wonder at his power or respect for his authority.

Luke 8:40–56

Now when Jesus returned, a crowd welcomed him, for they were all expecting him. Then a man named Jairus, a ruler of the synagogue, came and fell at Jesus' feet, pleading with him to come to his house because his only daughter, a girl of about twelve, was dying. As Jesus was on his way, the crowds almost crushed him. And a woman was there who had been subject to bleeding for twelve years, but no one could heal her. She came up behind him and touched the edge of his cloak, and immediately her bleeding stopped. "Who touched me?" Jesus asked. When they all denied it, Peter said, "Master, the people are crowding and pressing against you." But Jesus said, "Someone touched me; I know that power has gone out from me." Then the woman, seeing that she could not go unnoticed, came trembling and fell at his feet. In the presence of all the people, she told why she had touched him and how she had been instantly healed. Then he said to her, "Daughter your faith has healed you. Go in peace." While Jesus was still speaking, someone came from the house of Jairus, the synagogue ruler. "Your daughter is dead," he said. "Don't bother the teacher any more." Hearing this, Jesus said to Jairus, "Don't be afraid; just believe, and she will be healed." When he arrived at the house of Jairus, he did not let anyone go in with him except Peter, John and James, and the child's father and mother. Meanwhile, all the people were wailing and mourning for her. "Stop wailing," Jesus said. "She is not dead but asleep." They laughed at him, knowing that she was dead. But he took her by the hand and said, "My child, get up!" Her spirit returned, and at once she stood up. Then Jesus told them to give her something to eat. Her parents were astonished, but he ordered them not to tell anyone what had happened. {NIV}

In need of healing, some reach out to touch Jesus. I imagine the bleeding woman, isolated, afraid, creeping through the crowd to get close without being noticed. I relate to her inadequacy and her need to be near the healer. I appreciate her humble belief that she could be healed, without being a bother, if she could just touch the Messianic tassels on his clothing. I watch her, and I cannot help but empathize with her attraction. He is irresistible, and fascinating, the Lord from whom neither she nor I can divert our eyes.

Some, like Jairus, lift others to touch Jesus. I envision Jairus, dejected, fearful, hurrying through the crowd to gain Jesus' attention in any way possible. I sympathize with his helplessness and his need to lay his girl at the feet of the Divine. I understand his submission when he walks with Jesus to visit a daughter he knows to be dead. In our weakness, the Christ offers the only answer. We cannot protect, so we entrust to the Creator's care those whom we cherish.

As Heavenly Father, Jesus comes with healing hands. I picture him, gentle and patient, pausing to remind the healed woman that she could go in peace. I see him comforting Jairus as he marches toward the stricken daughter. For those unwilling to come, Jesus will search. For those unable to come, Jesus will travel. Almighty God has arrived to make your suffering his suffering, your burden his own and your deliverance his business.

A magnificent web stretches to gather in my soul. Glistening and beautiful, it shimmers in the morning light as the dew drips to the ground. It stretches across the expanse of my life, reaching every corner of my existence. Some strands my prayers put in place. Others have strung strands with their prayers for my well-being. Most strands God has woven himself, searching for me, calling my name, and pursuing me anywhere I could be found. As I follow him down his path, his gaze is unyielding, his purpose is immutable, and his grip is unbreakable.

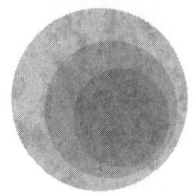

Luke 9:18–20

> And it happened that while He was praying alone, the disciples were with Him, and He questioned them, saying, "Who do the people say that I am?" They answered and said, "John the Baptist, and others say Elijah; but others, that one of the prophets of old has risen again." And He said to them, "But who do you say that I am?" And Peter answered and said, "The Christ of God." {NASB}

Sometimes I struggle with the question of whether God exists. Uncomfortable with the intangible, improperly named *supernatural*, I resist belief in anything beyond what I can see, feel, hear, touch, or otherwise experience with my five senses. The empiricist within me plagues my soul and haunts my dreams. I fear death more than any other evil, even hell, because I can envision nothing more damning than eternal emptiness. I so greatly fear death because I cannot tangibly *prove* that the ephemeral soul is truly immortal. Nudging against the silence of oblivion, a voice whispers, "Who do you say I am?"

Two thousand years later the question, "Who is Jesus?" is still sufficiently pressing to grace the cover of *Time* magazine. Even among those who reject empiricism and atheism, the answer is disheartening. Muslims, Buddhists, Jews, and Hindus revere Jesus as a great prophet or enlightened man, but they will not bow a knee to Jesus as Lord and Messiah. The world contorts in anger at Jesus' claim that "No one comes to the Father except through me." Society refuses to admit Jesus to the Deity Club unless he accepts his rightful place as one among equals in the pantheon of gods. While Jesus alone paid the unimaginable price for his claim to exclusive allegiance, the world ridicules Christ for his perceived arrogance, intolerance, and closed-mindedness. The demons of Islam, eastern religion, and secularism conspire to brand Jesus as a liar. Yet, through the clanging of false prophesy, from cleric and secularist alike, even such an institution as *Time* magazine cannot shake the now centuries-old question, "Who do you say I am?"

My Christian friends also struggle with the question, "Who is Jesus?" While they claim Jesus as personal Savior, they do not acknowledge him as Lord. They relegate him to afterthought when they deliberately choose sin, adopt secular ideals, or assert ownership rather than stewardship over money. It is foolish to recognize Jesus as God and reject him as King. While such an irrational conclusion cannot withstand the light of Scripture, the devaluation of Jesus creeps into their lives. They neither intentionally repudiate him nor consciously banish him, but slowly succumb as personal will replaces prayer as the determinative value. However, innumerable radically-changed lives answer the persistent voice questioning, "Who do you say I am?"

I can never escape him, nor would I if I could. Neither time nor religions nor philosophies nor wars nor famine nor pestilence have silenced Jesus' enduring question. Whether I continue to fight empiricism or some other false teaching or personal rebellion, the Holy Spirit will chase me, all the way to Nineveh if need be, to repeat the question, "Who do you say I am?" I will not experience peace and quiet until the words of my lips, the thoughts of my head, the desires of my heart, and the acts of my hands testify that Jesus is "the Christ of God."

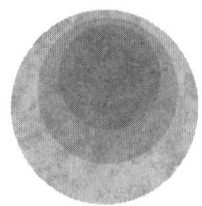

Luke 9:28–31

> About eight days later Jesus took Peter, John, and James with him and went up on a mountain to pray. While he was praying, his face changed, and his clothes became shining white. Suddenly Moses and Elijah were there speaking with him. They appeared in heavenly glory and talked about all that Jesus' death in Jerusalem would mean. {CEV}

It was summer vacation when, driven by spiritual thirst and parental expectations, I attended evening church services with my family. That night, I was awestruck by a young woman who had not previously visited my church. I glanced over; she glanced back; my mind raced and the rest of the service was a defeat for the Kingdom of God. After the service, I secluded myself away with my friends, sure that I would never see this girl again. She was just a visitor, a lonely stranger in the spiritual night. But suddenly I realized to my discomfort that the only people remaining were my family, the mysterious stranger, and her family.

Trying to hide my nervousness, I hung mutely at the edge of the group. Then, her dad turned to me and addressed me by name. To my horror he asked not the innocuous inquiries of unfamiliarity, but the now-dangerous questions of personal acquaintance. What had I done? To whom was I talking? This seemed like a much better idea when she was forever to be far away, and I could be a fool without consequence. This man knew me. After ten minutes of flipping through pictures in my head, I realized that I had spent this Lord's Day flirting with a friend's younger sister. My discomfort culminated when I was formally introduced to the object of my embarrassment.

Others may be skeptical, but such experiences convince me that I am the victim of a conspiracy by Gabriel, Michael, and other unnamed angels, who at points of leisure set me up to embarrass myself, arranging such scenarios for their enjoyment and relaxation. In the service of a Lord who commands a seventh day of rest, there must be ample respite from battling Satan's hosts to subject me to more than one cosmic practical joke. Does God not laugh when we laugh, just as he suffers when we do? Does he not find pleasure in our happiness? In contrast to the heavenly vision portrayed by movies, the kingdom of God is a beehive of activity, worship, work, and entertainment. The kingdom reflects restoration of creation, including the humor innate in us creatures, as it would have been if forever uncorrupted by sin. No offense to either cloud enthusiasts or musicians partial to harp, but the cartoon version of heaven would bore me.

I am also pleased that Moses and Elijah, even hundreds of years after Moses' death and Elijah's ascension, have rejected any temptation to "rest in peace" in favor of active participation in God's redemptive plan. As Bill and Ted aptly noted in their excellent adventure, the righteous dudes do rock on. For whatever reason, God has chosen people to further his plan for redemption. Could the ultimate act of grace be that the very engine of creation's destruction, man, serves as a redemptive vehicle through Christ? Like Adam must have enjoyed working in unspoiled Eden, I eagerly await such a job, labor without mental stress or physical weariness, work that does not beg for the arrival of Friday afternoon. I am grateful to God, angel, and saint alike for their labor, and I do not for one minute begrudge them their fun at my expense.

Luke 9:37–43

On the next day, when they came down from the mountain, a large crowd met Him. And a man from the crowd shouted, saying, "Teacher, I beg You to look at my son, for he is my only boy, and a spirit seizes him, and he suddenly screams, and it throws him into a convulsion with foaming at the mouth; and only with difficulty does it leave him, mauling him as it leaves. I begged Your disciples to cast it out, and they could not." And Jesus answered and said, "You unbelieving and perverted generation, how long shall I be with you and put up with you? Bring your son here." While he was still approaching, the demon slammed him to the ground and threw him into a convulsion. But Jesus rebuked the unclean spirit, and healed the boy and gave him back to his father. And they were all amazed at the greatness of God. {NASB}

Does anybody really believe in demons? Do evil spirits actually possess people, throw boys into convulsions, and speak audibly to God's messengers? Has Frank Peretti entertained but not educated us with his wild tales of magnificent archangels leading God's host into battle against those fallen from heaven? Modern science scoffs at demons, seeing them as mythical creatures of psychosis and the church's desire for control. If such beings exist, our culture nervously minimizes them. No danger accompanies the mischievous red imp perched on Bugs Bunny's left shoulder or whispering in Homer Simpson's ear. No damage lies in the trail of the Halloween costume that just trampled through my flowerbeds in search of candy. Even if such beings are real or more than naughty, man claims superiority as we "Shout at the Devil" without fear and race up and down the "Highway to Hell." We worry little about laughing at the devil; we know from *Poltergeist*, *Ghostbusters*, *Seventh Sign*, *End of Days*, and *Devil's Advocate* that we will eventually triumph. Also, Daniel Webster, Marge Simpson, Jerry Lewis, and the Charlie Daniels Band have beaten the devil in Tennessee, Springfield, Washington D.C., and Georgia. Has not modern man evolved beyond the reach of superstition and evil spirits?

I must confess that not only do I believe in demons, but I

know my demons by name. I need not introduce you to my companion, Lust. No matter my situation, I refuse to content myself with God's gifts, and instead envy his gifts to others. I lack contentment, entertain impure thoughts, and I watch television and movies that have no place in my home. This demon has me good. Yet, I am not alone. From Jimmy Swaggert to any anonymous pastor, the demon Lust has strangled the life out of many dedicated, godly men.

Please meet a second, subtler member of my entourage, the demon Pride. I worry about my image, ignore God as benefactor, and exude conceit. Psychologists might claim that I suffer from an inferiority complex, but I believe my demonic pride to be the same that cast Lucifer from heaven.

My friends also run in interesting social circles. I have met their close friend, the demon Hate. They have courted Hate, and have drained their last remnants of love, joy, and peace in his service. Responding to reminders of past crimes, both real and imagined, they lock their arms tightly around Hate. They refuse to permit the embers of vengeance to die, as their spiritual Rasputin stokes their self-loathing or their anger against others. I have met the woman who sits alone in the back pew, refusing to socialize after the service. I naturally dislike her because the demons Depression and Loneliness drive her into the arms of the demon Hopelessness. Even though this vicious attack leaves her longing for death, she pushes away the Christian community, which, for whatever reason, lacks interest in rescuing her from her isolation.

I would like to say that all is well with my soul, but such a happy ending would be untrue. I hate myself for my enslavement to my demons. While I repeatedly resolve to cast these demons into hell, I find myself powerless to expel them. Paul states that we can do all things through Christ who strengthens us. I give intellectual assent to Paul, but I show no trust in his words. I am not alone. Drugs and alcohol, sex and selfishness, false religion and empty philosophy still asphyxiate the world's people. I think we can safely discredit the notion of the devil as a little red clown with a pitchfork.

Luke 9:43–45

> While everyone was still amazed at what Jesus was doing, he said to his disciples, "Pay close attention to what I am telling you! The Son of Man will be handed over to his enemies." But the disciples did not know what he meant. The meaning was hidden from them. They could not understand it, and they were afraid to ask. {CEV}

My friend Greg is the luckiest Yahtzee player ever. From prehistoric times, no man has ever received more from the hand of chance. Greg routinely rolls a 1, 2, 3, 5, and 6, which we will lightheartedly refer to as a "buckeye straight." Seeing the paltry opportunity for a "long straight," Greg picks up the 1 to roll for his elusive 4. I explain to Greg that he intends to embark on a fool's errand of probability, a mathematical miscalculation of the type that has financed so impressive a landmark as the Las Vegas strip. Greg sneers and spins the die. Up pops another 3. I nod knowingly, but Greg does not waver, picking up the same unlucky die and again flipping it on the table. It bounces around and then wobbles like a Weeble before the 4 makes its magical appearance. I fight back words unfit for publication as Greg calmly fills in long straight on his score pad. After obtaining a Yahtzee in similar fashion, Greg announces a score best measured in light years, and I complain that Greg does not get what he deserves.

As recounted in 1 Samuel 29, the Philistines attacked and routed Israel at Mount Gilboa. Among the dead was Jonathan, crown prince of Israel, and loyal friend of David. God struck down a man bound to David by covenant, the man who had protected from his own father the friend who would take his throne. On the slopes of Mount Gilboa, God also struck down Saul, the disobedient king who had defied the prophet Samuel. Jonathan died at the same time and in the same manner as his rebellious father. In the aftermath, David wept and fasted not only for his friend but also for the king who had wronged him. Israel mourned for both the angelic Jonathan and his defiant father. Neither Saul nor Jonathan got what they deserved.

The Gospels describe the ultimate in unfairness, the Son of Man being handed over to his enemies. Like kings, friends, and tax collectors of old, we do not receive from God that which we deserve. I may be obedient like Jonathan, but God does not see obedience as grounds for special privilege. The lifelong Christian receives the same gift that God gives to the last-minute penitent. I protest, claiming in vain that I offer more to God than Saul, or Greg, my disobedient—or merely lucky—friend, who stumbles blindly into blessing. Then I stop cold in my tracks as the Holy Spirit asks whether I really want what I deserve or what I can have because Jesus did not get what he deserved. My Jesus, my hopelessly unfair Jesus, listens patiently when I acknowledge that I offer nothing more than shattered dreams, broken promises, and embarrassing failures. In honest moments, I recognize that I contribute so much less than Jonathan, but I receive an equal portion from Jesus. So saint or sinner, Jonathan or Saul, priest or tax collector, seemingly cursed or unimaginably lucky, the Lord presumes to fashion his own plan to prosper his people. Regarding my future, I am almost afraid to ask, but I will never utter the words "that's not fair" to my heavenly Father.

Luke 9:46–50

An argument started among the disciples as to which of them would be the greatest. Jesus, knowing their thoughts, took a little child and had him stand beside him. Then he said to them, "Whoever welcomes this little child in my name welcomes me; and whoever welcomes me welcomes the one who sent me. For he who is least among you all—he is the greatest." "Master," said John, "we saw a man driving out demons in your name and we tried to stop him, because he is not one of us." "Do not stop him," Jesus said, "for whoever is not against you is for you." {NIV}

In high school, Bob Huizenga was certainly the greatest among us. A star on the basketball court, Bob regularly put on display his considerable skills and ferocious tenacity. Bob was not just an exceptional athlete, but also a good student and homecoming king. He was extraordinarily popular among parents and revered by students. As of high school graduation night, Bob intended to study and play basketball at Calvin College.

The next night, a drunk driver killed Bob while he was returning from his girlfriend's house. A small town went into shock. Even so impersonal a medium as the local newspaper managed to capture the tragedy and waste. His funeral belonged to the entire community, a day that brought words I have long forgotten but etched images permanently in my mind.

Over the years, I have thought often of Bob Huizenga. I know his success, fame, popularity, and greatness to be fleeting—each earthly treasure destroyed when his life ended in an instant. More significantly, I remember Bob as the greatest among us because he did not consider himself to be most important. My most vivid memories of Bob do not come from evenings spent dunking basketballs in the school gym. At the center of my memory is a humble individual, willing to give time and attention to anyone. I remember Bob's disinterest in the teenage social caste system. Nobody is perfect, but Bob did his best to be honorable, handling accomplishment with humility and being quick to share credit. There have been other popular basketball stars but none so appreciated or magnetic. I remember Bob as the most accomplished and the least proud among us. I remember a servant who humbly obeyed Christ. I miss Bob Huizenga, and I do not understand why God permitted the sin of another to take such a promising young life. However, I am richer for having known him, and I anticipate remaking our acquaintance.

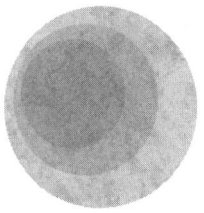

Luke 9:51–56

Now it came to pass, when the time had come for Him to be received up, that He steadfastly set His face to go to Jerusalem, and sent messengers before His face. And as they went, they entered a village of the Samaritans, to prepare for Him. But they did not receive Him, because His face was set for the journey to Jerusalem. And when His disciples James and John saw this, they said, "Lord, do You want us to command fire to come down from heaven and consume them, just as Elijah did?" But He turned and rebuked them, and said, "You do not know what manner of spirit you are of. For the Son of Man did not come to destroy men's lives but to save them." And they went to another village. {NKJV}

Although given every benefit of a decent upbringing, the students in my ninth grade shop class proved the accuracy of the Reformed doctrine of the total depravity of man. This collection of hooligans so greatly tormented the shop teacher that I can only imagine how that poor man must have begged God for early retirement. One fall day, my classmate Steve ground a four by four down to a wooden pole about three feet long and two inches thick. He then cut this pole in half. Perhaps with a purpose, perhaps with no ill-motive, Steve attached a chain between the two identical small poles, finishing with an artistically pleasing creation that bore more than a passing resemblance to numchucks. The shop teacher surprised Steve, asking, "What do you have there?" In a moment of genius, Steve's fingers held his creation dangling from the center of the chain as the words came quickly, "Wind chimes." "Wind chimes!" said our shop teacher. "What a great idea; we should all make wind chimes." Wind chimes gave way to Christmas ornaments (throwing stars) during our plastics unit, as my ninth grade shop class soon became Michigan's largest producer of illegal martial arts weapons. Detentions did not fly as they would have had my teacher been more astute in the Asiatic arts, or as they did when he outsmarted us with respect to other schemes and plots, but a teacher's lounge conversation at some point must have given this man reason to be very angry.

Ironically, the school assigned this same teacher, the victim of our betrayal in shop class, the responsibility to teach our Bible class. Notwithstanding the ebb and flow of the Shop Class War of 1984, this teacher arrived every fourth hour to tell the same group of hellions who tormented him in second hour that Jesus loved them. He refused to disown us despite our disrespectful attitudes and the embarrassment that we caused him. He likewise did not gloat on those days when numerous detentions served as a badge of honor commemorating his successful coordination of a ninth grade sting operation. Years of service to unappreciative youth wore him down, but no student left that class without knowing that both God and teacher cared.

Praise God that he is gracious and slow to anger. Just as Jesus sent messengers to prepare a Samaritan town for his arrival, I know that Jesus sent my long-suffering shop teacher to model forgiveness. I read that the disciples asked to rid themselves of the Samaritan people that did not welcome Jesus to their town, and I suspect that my shop teacher, upon learning the true nature of our actions, in moments of weakness, fervently wished to call fire from heaven to consume us students. Yet, who gets the rebuke? Is it the disrespectful hellions of the Bruce Lee Wannabe Club? No, it is the mild-mannered shop teacher, the faithful disciple, for whom Jesus has words of correction. Jesus instructs my shop teacher that he must forgive our treachery, as well as that other incident involving a thermostat, a small pile of snow, and a grossly overheated classroom. And I know my shop teacher did just what he was told, displaying the remarkable grace by which God forgives any rebellion, no matter the severity. I fear the overwhelming responsibility that I inherit as I transition from student to proverbial shop teacher. Out there is a shop teacher, an art teacher, a German teacher, and at least two music teachers, to whom I owe an apology. But I thank God that I also owe them gratitude for modeling Christian forgiveness.

Luke 10:21–24

At that very time He rejoiced greatly in the Holy Spirit, and said, "I praise You, O Father, Lord of heaven and earth, that You have hidden these things from the wise and intelligent and have revealed them to infants. Yes, Father, for this way was well-pleasing in Your sight. All things have been handed over to Me by My Father, and no one knows who the Son is except the Father, and who the Father is except the Son, and anyone to whom the Son wills to reveal Him." Turning to the disciples, He said privately, "Blessed are the eyes which see the things you see, for I say to you, that many prophets and kings wished to see the things which you see, and did not see them, and to hear the things which you hear, and did not hear them." {NASB}

My heart yearns for purpose in the universe, to shed the haunting doubt that all is futile, to silence the existentialist's mocking laughter. With an explorer's zeal, I search for life's meaning in sports, academia, and social attention. My efforts as a philosophical Christopher Columbus or a metaphysical Amerigo Vespucci produce zilch, establishing only that I judge life poorly. I think that age or experience or education will answer my most perplexing questions. But neither the elderly nor the adventuresome nor the scholarly offer me insight. Instead, I, along with them, stare dumbfounded into the darkness. Unable to resist the black hopelessness that envelops my soul, *Pilgrim's Stagnation* rather than *Pilgrim's Progress* best encapsulates my autobiography.

Sin fogs my vision as I peer through the lens of earthly power. My binoculars, namely money, authority, and influence, illuminate nothing, forcing me to enlist the world's best guides. These escorts have previously served the wise, rich, and kingly. Carl Sagan offers billions and billions of years of cosmology so that I might know my origins. Liberal democracy instructs me to trust my government as the surest means to a safe journey. When bad things happen to good people, the United Way and the Chicago School of Economics suggest ways to ease my conscience and distance myself from suffering. When I wonder why anything matters, I remember a rumor that children are our future, so teach them well and let them lead the way. Yet all of the world's collective wisdom provides neither hope nor meaning.

Thank God for revealing his kingdom to children—those the world deems unlearned and unimportant. Since worldly ignorance covers my eyes, I praise God that I need not search for him in some cosmic Easter egg hunt. God does not cast the earthly privileged from heaven, but neither will he substitute the silliness of humanist cosmology for Jesus' payment for sin. If I want to enter the Kingdom of God, and if I have no shirt and no shoes, well, no problem. If I have no Jesus, it is no entry, no way, no how. The world says, "What foolishness to place your hope there." Should I trust in their wisdom as I lie broken on the sidewalk? No, I reach only for my Lord, because "all the king's horses and all the king's men cannot put Humpty together again."

Luke 10:25–37

On one occasion an expert in the law stood up to test Jesus. "Teacher," he asked, "what must I do to inherit eternal life?" "What is written in the Law?" he replied. "How do you read it?" He answered: "'Love the Lord your God with all your heart and with all your soul and with all your strength and with all your mind'; and, 'Love your neighbor as yourself.'" "You have answered correctly," Jesus replied. "Do this and you will live." But he wanted to justify himself, so he asked Jesus, "And who is my neighbor?" In reply Jesus said: "A man was going down from Jerusalem to Jericho, when he fell into the hands of robbers. They stripped him of his clothes, beat him and went away, leaving him half dead. A priest happened to be going down the same road, and when he saw the man, he passed by on the other side. So too, a Levite, when he came to the place and saw him, passed by on the other side. But a Samaritan, as he traveled, came where the man was; and when he saw him, he took pity on him. He went to him and bandaged his wounds, pouring on oil and wine. Then he put the man on his own donkey, took him to an inn and took care of him. The next day he took out two silver coins and gave them to the innkeeper. 'Look after him,' he said, 'and when I return, I will reimburse you for any extra expense you may have.' Which of these three do you think was a neighbor to the man who fell into the hands of robbers?" The expert in the law replied, "The one who had mercy on him." Jesus told him, "Go and do likewise." {NIV}

The expert in the law has outlined an obtainable set of criteria for love: I should love the Lord my God with all my heart, soul, and mind, and I should love my neighbor as myself. Despite my failures, I can love the Lord my God—I easily love my Creator and Redeemer. I think I can also love humankind, though I confess more than a little empathy with Linus Van Pelt's apt paraphrase of Dostoevsky's statement: "I love mankind; it's people I can't stand." I do not fret when I consider my obligation to love my narrowly-defined neighbor, those whom I like and with whom I voluntarily associate. My fingertips tingle with easily summoned mercy for my beloved family and dear friends.

Jesus has a different idea in mind. He envisions a Samaritan who assists his enemy, a broken Jew lying along the dangerous, narrow mountain path known as the Jericho road. Not content to merely introduce the Jews to their new Samaritan neighbors, Jesus insists that love transcend emotional sympathy to touch a bloody mess. The Samaritan jeopardizes his personal safety by lingering. He endangers his health by battling through the flies, sacrifices his religious purity by laying his hands on this unclean creature, and lightens his purse by paying the innkeeper for the Jew's recuperation.

I hear echoes of this injured Jew in the cries of our own homosexual community, which lies beaten down by AIDS along the Jericho road. Just as Samaritan history offended Jewish sensibility, the gay agenda attacks the Christian social order, undermines God's rule, and offends moral decency. A Christian who associates with homosexuals risks physical harm from the hands of hate-mongers and jeopardizes personal safety by assisting an AIDS patient with physical touch. When a Christian church empties its coffers to pay medical bills or household costs it forgoes the perception of piety in the community by befriending those so easily branded as sinners. Consistent with the parable, Jesus says, "So what? I want you to be Samaritans to all those broken along the Jericho road." For Jesus, the merely neighborly Samaritan extends mercy beyond his friends and relatives to reach his worst enemy. While the task appears daunting, I too can, with God's redemptive power, reside in Mr. Jesus' Neighborhood.

Luke 10:38–42

As Jesus and the disciples continued on their way to Jerusalem, they came to a village where a woman named Martha welcomed them into her home. Her sister, Mary, sat at the Lord's feet, listening to what he taught. But Martha was worrying over the big dinner she was preparing. She came to Jesus and said, "Lord, doesn't it seem unfair to you that my sister just sits here while I do all the work? Tell her to come and help me." But the Lord said to her, "My dear Martha, you are so upset over all these details! There is really only one thing worth being concerned about. Mary has discovered it—and I won't take it away from her." {NLT}

It was a perfect Michigan summer day when my girlfriend's father lowered his boat into the water. The wind whipped through my hair as we sped away from the marina along Lake Michigan's magnificent shores. The sun sparkled on the blue water. The white sand dunes towered over the crashing waves. What could be better than cruising past picturesque sights? What better way to spend a summer day than racing over water and splashing through waves?

Suddenly, my girlfriend's father cut the throttle. Did we run out of gas? Was he sick? None of my fears came to fruition. Rather, he had erroneously concluded that now was the time to haul out the cleaner and scrub the nearly spotless boat. My girlfriend and her sisters lay out in the sun as if this horrible change of fortune was expected and normal. A menial chore had reduced a racehorse of a boat and the strong sea breezes to a bobbing, piney-fresh test tube for seasickness.

In our chores and organization, we can forget our purpose. The story of Mary and Martha reminds me of a wedding, supposedly the most important day of one's life, which is ruined by familial attempts to preserve the moment. Amidst the pageantry, an army of cameramen poorly camouflage themselves in the flowers. They jump over guests and join the bride and her father in their once-in-a-lifetime walk down the aisle. Meanwhile, the videographer spins to catch the groom's reaction, only to tag Grandma in the jaw with the camera. This zeal to capture the magic guarantees that the event itself is scarred, if not lost.

Jesus' friend, Martha, was an organized hostess. The Monica Gellar of biblical times, she had prepared accommodations and meals—everything necessary for her guests' comfort. By way of contrast, Mary refused to plan or help with arrangements for Jesus' stay. Yet, Jesus chided Martha for her worry.

Jesus did not correct Martha for her foresight but for the fact that her foresight blurred her *now*-sight. Martha hosted God's son but did not take time to enjoy him or soak it all in. She was so concerned that her party succeed, she forgot to spend time with her guests. Mary chose better, not because she was unhelpful, but because she took advantage of her short time with Jesus.

My life often resembles Martha's story. I rush from event to event, scurrying to make plans to such an extent that I do not stop to enjoy fellowship with God. As I think of the passing years, college seems like a blur, law school is really fuzzy, and I realize that I have now held my job for some time. I dedicate precious little time to God. My earthly stay is short, a limited blessing, and I waste my days rushing about at the expense of a rich relationship with God. So far, Mary has chosen wiser than I have chosen. While planning ahead may be good stewardship, I hope that I will choose better the next time that Jesus comes to visit.

Luke 11:1–13

One day Jesus was praying in a certain place. When he finished, one of his disciples said to him, "Lord, teach us to pray, just as John taught his disciples." He said to them, "When you pray, say: 'Father, hallowed be your name, your kingdom come. Give us each day our daily bread. Forgive us our sins, for we also forgive everyone who sins against us. And lead us not into temptation.'" Then he said to them, "Suppose one of you has a friend, and he goes to him at midnight and says, 'Friend, lend me three loaves of bread, because a friend of mine on a journey has come to me, and I have nothing to set before him.' Then the one inside answers, 'Don't bother me. The door is already locked, and my children are with me in bed. I can't get up and give you anything.' I tell you, though he will not get up and give him the bread because he is his friend, yet because of the man's boldness he will get up and give him as much as he needs. So I say to you: Ask and it will be given to you; seek and you will find; knock and the door will be opened to you. For everyone who asks receives; he who seeks finds; and to him who knocks, the door will be opened. Which of you fathers, if your son asks for a fish, will give him a snake instead? Or if he asks for an egg, will give him a scorpion? If you then, though you are evil, know how to give good gifts to your children, how much more will your Father in heaven give the Holy Spirit to those who ask him!" {NIV}

I am grateful that Jesus has taught me to properly pray to the Most High God. As Luke recites the Lord's Prayer, Jesus explains the appropriate subject matter and intense power of prayer. I pray best when I cling to the Lord's Prayer. I begin with "Our Father who art in heaven, Hallowed be thy name." I then request that I and others would respect God. I continue with "Thy kingdom come. Thy will be done, on earth as it is in heaven." My mind spins with faces and names as I ask the Good Shepherd to find every lost sheep. I work through the entire prayer, meditating on each phrase until, guided by the Lord's example, I have prayed about everything worthy of prayer. I should not be admired for the vibrancy of my shamefully neglected prayer life. Jesus' prayer serves as the backdrop for the best of my prayers.

A terrific story immediately follows as God reminds us to be relentless, even obnoxious, in our prayer life. We should set aside tepid and sniveling prayers, instead asking for magnificent things in Jesus' name. While we possess great spiritual authority, we receive our hearts' desires only when we devote our efforts to kingdom riches. Prayer for worldly treasure serves no useful purpose. A kingdom that grows through humble weakness needs no worldly power to sustain its prosperity. We should not carelessly spill prayer on earthly trinkets and party favors.

By way of contrast, true spiritual intercession gives me great riches. I do not often enough approach God, but I am spiritually wealthy because relatives, friends, and church members have sought God on my behalf. They have spent hours reminding God that he has promised to remember me and pledged to snatch me from sin's grip. Most importantly, Jesus has wept at God's throne regarding my lost state. He has searched me out, knocked at God's door, and pointed to the nail prints in his hands and feet as sufficient payment for my soul. I am safe in the hands of a loving father who listens to his son.

Luke 11:14–28

Jesus was driving out a demon that was mute. When the demon left, the man who had been mute spoke, and the crowd was amazed. But some of them said, "By Beelzebub, the prince of demons, he is driving out demons." Others tested him by asking for a sign from heaven. Jesus knew their thoughts and said to them: "Any kingdom divided against itself will be ruined, and a house divided against itself will fall. If Satan is divided against himself, how can his kingdom stand? I say this because you claim that I drive out demons by Beelzebub. Now if I drive out demons by Beelzebub, by whom do your followers drive them out? So then, they will be your judges. But if I drive out demons by the finger of God, then the kingdom of God has come to you. When a strong man, fully armed, guards his own house, his possessions are safe. But when someone stronger attacks and overpowers him, he takes away the armor in which the man trusted and divides up the spoils. He who is not with me is against me, and he who does not gather with me, scatters. When an evil spirit comes out of a man, it goes through arid places seeking rest and does not find it. Then it says, 'I will return to the house I left.' When it arrives, it finds the house swept clean and put in order. Then it goes and takes seven other spirits more wicked than itself, and they go in and live there. And the final condition of that man is worse than the first." As Jesus was saying these things, a woman in the crowd called out, "Blessed is the mother who gave you birth and nursed you." He replied, "Blessed rather are those who hear the word of God and obey it." {NIV}

As Midwesterners, my friends knew no place greater than Cedar Point, the king of amusement parks. They regaled me with tales of breathtaking drops, tremendous speed, face-squishing G-forces, and an endless selection of roller coasters. They described rides so high and fast that they risked instantaneous death when the feeble restraining harness clicked into place. Each buddy finished his story with the phrase, "Dude, you gotta go next summer." I smiled, gave some non-committal response, and hid the fact that I am deathly afraid of heights.

I live my Christian life on a roller coaster, with soaring peaks of dedication to God followed by deep valleys of spiritual disinterest. As worldly values creep in, I compromise about a sexually explicit movie, a profane book, a violent television show, a hedonistic concert, or an alcohol-soaked party. I leave the spiritual mountaintop because I want my MTV. I rationalize my behavior as keeping me in touch with the lost world. After all, I listen to Britney Spears, but I am not dating her. The party represents a witnessing opportunity, and Jesus did spend time with prostitutes and other sinners. I rationalize that I do not imitate the violence or sexual lifestyle aggrandized by movies or music, or permit my speech to include the harshest available language. Buying the lie that I can justify my divided loyalty, I claim that I need worldly exposure to prepare for Christian service.

The saints praise the magnificent view from the spiritual mountaintop, so why do I instead plummet ninety-five miles per hour into the pit. Sometimes my spiritual roller coaster dips so quickly that my stomach drops. Other times my coaster weaves gently as I descend downward unaware. Sin undermines my commitment to God and robs others of the service I could give to Christ.

The world blinds me to truth, and convinces me that I sufficiently love others by merely shunning violent acts, or that chastity is less about maintaining mental purity than abstaining from sexual acts. I limit my cursing rather than speaking only to glorify God or to uplift those he loves. I stumble through life, never controlling my response to temptation. Every time I halfheartedly clean my heart, my demons return with reinforcements. Each repetition saps my strength until I am discouraged.

I must prayerfully overcome my fear of spiritual heights. I need to fill my life with goodness and purity to keep myself devoted to Jesus. Only when my house is undivided, will it stand. I pray for a heart that goes full blast for the Lord, leaving no room for Satan to divide my allegiance. Until then, I will bumble along waiting for the next heart-stopping drop; but he never lets me crash. Instead, when all seems lost, I always hear that precious sound that foretells restoration, clickity clackity, clickity clackity, clickity clackity, click.

Luke 11:33–36

"No one lights a lamp and puts it in a place where it will be hidden, or under a bowl. Instead he puts it on its stand, so that those who come in may see the light. Your eye is the lamp of your body. When your eyes are good, your whole body also is full of light. But when they are bad, your body also is full of darkness. See to it, then, that the light within you is not darkness. Therefore, if your whole body is full of light, and no part of it dark, it will be completely lighted, as when the light of a lamp shines on you." {NIV}

Almost everyone who has grown up as a Christian can hum "This Little Light of Mine," a Sunday school anthem so familiar that General Electric has used it for television commercials.

Even now, many years after the second grade, I can still do the motions.

> *This little light of mine,*
> *I'm gonna let it shine.*

Christians inherently understand the truth behind "This Little Light of Mine." Are our minds not spiritual reflectors of our hearts? Are our actions not an echo of that which we have seen and heard? Parents admonish their children saying, "Be careful little eyes what you see. Be careful little ears what you hear," and "Be careful little feet where you go." However charming, Sunday school lessons and Bible-camp songs do not tell us how challenging it is to absorb enough light to be a suitable reflector.

As a teenager in the days of big hair, parachute pants, turned-up collars, and, dare we say, one earring, light for reflection was scarce indeed. The price of social admission included rebellion and hedonism that squelched any escaping glimmer of Jesus. Satan brazenly raised his head, stared into our eyes, and mocked any heart that would not embrace the darkness. Creatures of the 1980s succumbed to the darkness, and the wonder drug cocaine, self-indulgence and greed, none of which reflected any light.

After Oliver Stone's *Wall Street* and then Nirvana's *Smells Like Teen Spirit* exposed the emptiness of excess, the devil changed gears and struck down the grunge generation by introducing them to hopelessness. The glitzy hedonist who had headlined the laser-dependent stage show called the 1980s evolved into the flannel-covered manic-depressive of the 1990s. Society ushered out David Lee Roth and welcomed Curt Cobain. The molten metal that had enthusiastically received the darkness gave way to depressed tones that questioned whether light or dark existed and denied that the distinction mattered. While the hedonist loved the darkness, this new force embraced an illusory enlightenment of relativism. With a new term, "political correctness," a culture dismissed the one true light, instead condemning *intolerance*—a code word for the notion that one must bend to the view that all *ideas* are created equal—as the 1990s' only unforgivable sin. My university likewise demanded subservience to toleration for all except those deemed to be intolerant. Believers in light were pushed to the communal periphery.

As September 11, 2001 forced a stunned country to acknowledge a real distinction between good and evil, Satan again changed tactics and imposed an equally insidious civil religion of dusk. The evil one permitted us to know *of God* so long as we did not know *God*. Our culture admitted that we could detect a god in the dim shadows but would not permit us to open the shade so that the sunlight would reveal his true nature. Our public discourse acknowledged dependency upon a hazy and distant god, who could be Allah or Jehovah or Buddha or the Great Spirit or whoever might fill in the void. However, few if any political figures named Jesus, or made reference to Islamic darkness. God could no longer be ignored, but Americans could minimize him to irrelevance. In this new manifestation of our civil religion, Satan appointed God to be the equivalent of president of the Soviet Union—a figurehead who greeted heads of state but who had only ceremonial authority. America chose a dim light of dusk just bright enough to see light but not so bright that we had to discern the landscape of truth.

While "This Little Light of Mine" is fabulous for young and old alike, we must not deceive ourselves that becoming effective spiritual reflectors will be easy. Worldly forces would like to fill us with evil darkness, or the murky powerlessness of dusk. The same world that rejects Christians as intolerant wants to influence our behavior. Media invades our lives, chewing up space and time that should be dedicated to good things. Our government and schools do not cast light to be reflected by students, but instead fill them with the darkness of godless evolution, safe sex, and the rest of the dregs of secular humanism. It takes prayer, obedience, and study of scripture to gather enough light to cast a proper reflection. When little light comes in, little light reflects to others. However, we praise God that where Jesus bursts from the heart, a great beacon of truth stabs through the darkness probing, reaching, and searching for the lost.

Luke 12:13–21

Someone in the crowd said to Him, "Teacher, tell my brother to divide the family inheritance with me." But He said to him, "Man, who appointed Me a judge or arbitrator over you?" Then He said to them, "Beware, and be on your guard against every form of greed; for not even when one has an abundance does his life consist of his possessions." And He told them a parable, saying, "The land of a rich man was very productive. And he began reasoning to himself, saying, 'What shall I do, since I have no place to store my crops?' Then he said, 'This is what I will do: I will tear down my barns and build larger ones, and there I will store all my grain and my goods. And I will say to my soul, "Soul, you have many goods laid up for many years to

> come; take your ease, eat, drink and be merry.'" But God said to him, 'You fool! This very night your soul is required of you; and now who will own what you have prepared?' So is the man who stores up treasure for himself, and is not rich toward God." {NASB}

In high school my friend measured his expenditure of money in terms of the number of compact discs that he could buy with the same funds. We would invite him out for pizza, and he would reply that pizza cost eight dollars, the equivalent of one CD. Although it tasted great, pizza's pleasures lasted but an evening in comparison to the lifetime of enjoyment that accompanied each new CD.

Consistent with my friend's balancing fortune that lasts, versus fortune that fades away, Jesus suggests that I should not accumulate earthly treasures in place of a relationship with God. No matter the worldly treasure, whether money, family, pleasure, fame, or friends; I would be foolish to reject God for one of these. Only the Pizza Hut investor, one who chases a reward that will be consumed, welcomes temporal idols to replace the Heavenly King. So-called great men grasp at eternal significance through such silly enterprises as empires, fortunes, memoirs, or my personal favorite, the presidential historical legacy. Do more people remember Hammurabi for his code of laws or his status as the Babylonian character in Sid Meier's classic computer game *Civilization III*? Does Hammurabi care? God sees them as the fools competing for the biggest barn. When Jesus refused to settle the inheritance dispute, he suggests not an absence of authority to judge, but an absence of interest in the outcome. Others will some day divide my possessions or throw them in a trash container, one like the dumpster that makes its symbolically rich appearance on a deceased grandparent's driveway. I will take only the blessings of each day lived for Jesus as if there will be no additional days. It seems so obvious, yet my spiritual closet spills over with clutter.

Satan has sold many people the carpe diem mentality. Young people live hell bent for leather, uncertain about whether tomorrow will come and unconcerned about whether it does. Hollywood depresses me with radically existential films, such as *Thelma and Louise*, where two women, portrayed as heroes, possess to the end nothing of any spiritual value. *Pulp Fiction* suggests that life is so randomly cruel and ironic that one must live for the immediate moment. *City of Angels* teaches us that tomorrow's blessings should be cast away for today's emotions. Twenty-first century America has a Pizza Hut on every corner.

Luke 12:49–53

"I have come to cast fire upon the earth; and how I wish it were already kindled! But I have a baptism to undergo, and how distressed I am until it is accomplished! Do you suppose that I came to grant peace on earth? I tell you, no, but rather division; for from now on five members in one household will be divided, three against two and two against three. They will be divided, father against son and son against father, mother against daughter and daughter against mother, mother-in-law against daughter-in-law and daughter-in-law against mother-in-law." {NASB}

Intellectual giant C. S. Lewis states that Jesus holds one of three possible identities: Lord or liar or lunatic. It seems to me that *Lord* or *lied about* are more refined alternatives. The Gospels identify Jesus as Lord because his life correlates to the Jewish teachings about the Messiah. No person, much less a lunatic, could time, shape, or fake events so as to satisfy the messianic requirements. There is no middle ground. Either the gospel writer has served as a faithful historian describing a Jesus who must be Messiah in light of Jewish doctrine, or he has lied to us about this same man and these same historical events. We must choose. Is he Lord—a title that requires that we obey? Or is he lied about—a historical curiosity who can be safely ignored?

Our society tries to avoid the question, bristling at each mention of the name Christ, a title that demands the community reach a decision. Unwilling to crown Jesus Lord, but reluctant to call Luke a liar, society ignores the historical, divisive Jesus who challenged the temple authority and claimed to be the Son of God. They would make him irrelevant by labeling him good (no liar involved) but overreaching in his claim (no Lord present, either). They prefer the ideology of *Star Trek* where the utopian Federation promotes universal harmony through mutual understanding. The Prime Directive, applicable to any man "going where no man has gone before," requires that the humanist explorer refrain from questioning another's beliefs. Let each believe what he would choose so long as he sincerely believes something short of absolute truth, saying as Shaquille O'Neal once responded to a sports reporter's question, "It is like the Pythagorean theorem, it has no answer." Let each person discover limitless available options but no required decisions.

Notwithstanding this attempt to marginalize Jesus, we must choose between Jesus as historical Lord and Jesus as lied about by Luke. Jesus insists that the world choose. There is no place on the ballot for Jesus as a good man who is irrelevant to me. It is the disciple of Jeffersonian liberty rather than messianic devotion that sees gray. So do I choose *Lord* or *lied about*? I must courageously say the answer is C squared.

Luke 12:54–59

Then Jesus turned to the crowd and said, "When you see clouds beginning to form in the west, you say, 'Here comes a shower.' And you are right. When the south wind blows, you say, 'Today will be a scorcher.' And it is. You hypocrites! You know how to interpret the appearance of the earth and the sky, but you can't interpret these present times. Why can't you decide for yourselves what is right? If you are on the way to court and you meet your accuser, try to settle the matter before it reaches the judge, or you may be sentenced and handed over to an officer and thrown in jail. And if that happens, you won't be free again until you have paid the last penny." {NLT}

In the United States, we understand weather. We speculate about it, we predict it, and we talk about it endlessly, especially when we have nothing else to say. Our NBC affiliate interrupts our regularly scheduled programming with a color radar report if so much as a moonbeam twinkles into the viewing area. While a European of the middle ages might have burned at the stake for hazarding a guess about the weather, we embrace Doppler radar, fund the National Weather Service, and turn loose meteorologists by the thousands on local television and radio. In contrast to theology, social convention has elevated weather to the pinnacle of subjects about which Americans can safely and knowledgeably converse.

In the United States, we do not understand eschatology or what we call the end times. While two thousand years have greatly improved weather forecasting, neither theologians nor laymen can forecast God's arrival. Used bookstores burst at the seams with works predicting an 80 percent chance of year 2000 rapture, a prediction, as it turns out, without basis. My agnostic friends admit that a loving God may exist, but nothing compels them to pursue a personal relationship with Jesus. Christians prove to be only a little more insightful, as we struggle to observe God guiding and interacting with this world.

How can we be so wise about weather and so foolish about God? Jesus must wonder about our fascination with weather in comparison to our lackadaisical attitude regarding the comings and goings of God Almighty. We move away from the Conqueror, despite his victory over sin that rains down our heads. We bask in the warmth of blessing, but we miss the sun that reminds us that

God loves and redeems his creation. We wander aimlessly, despite the thunderheads that urge us to seek the Lord's shelter. As this spiritual storm rages, why do I hide under the covers? I ignore the maelstrom, and, despite the windblown rain that beats against my body, I raise my moistened finger in the hope of detecting a breeze in the air. ●

Luke 13:1–9

Now there were some present at that time who told Jesus about the Galileans whose blood Pilate had mixed with their sacrifices. Jesus answered, "Do you think that these Galileans were worse sinners than all the other Galileans because they suffered this way? I tell you, no! But unless you repent, you too will all perish. Or those eighteen who died when the tower in Siloam fell on them—do you think they were more guilty than all the others living in Jerusalem? I tell you, no! But unless you repent, you too will all perish." Then he told this parable: "A man had a fig tree, planted in his vineyard, and he went to look for fruit on it, but did not find any. So he said to the man who took care of the vineyard, 'For three years now I've been coming to look for fruit on this fig tree and haven't found any. Cut it down! Why should it use up the soil?' 'Sir,' the man replied, 'leave it alone for one more year, and I'll dig around it and fertilize it. If it bears fruit next year, fine! If not, then cut it down.'"

{NIV}

I sometimes catch myself holding God accountable to our notion that people should get what they deserve. We say, "Life is not fair," a proverb that translates as "God is not fair." In our private thoughts, we wonder why he has subjected us to some loss or cause for complaint. I remember a high-school classmate who was murdered in front of a grocery store. I remain baffled over how this woman's death has advanced God's kingdom even one inch. The residents of the Cleveland Clinic pediatric oncology ward and the occupants of the nearby Ronald McDonald House can testify that people do not always get what they deserve.

While God disciplines his children, he refuses to bend to karma. Neither does he connect an obedient life to temporal blessing. As a child, I would complain to my mother with the phrase, "That is not fair." She would invariably respond, "Well, life is not fair." I would reply, "Yes, but shouldn't you do your best to make life as fair as possible?" While my mother has never replied to my question, God answers my inquiry with a resounding no. Jesus says that those whom he embraces at the last breath of a wicked life receive the same reward as those who serve faithfully for many years. We do not get what we pay for with God.

I nevertheless poison my faith with superstition regarding divine karma. I pretend that I receive all things in life, good or ill, as a result of good or rebellious behavior. I interpret every negative turn as vengeance for sin. I consider every blessing to be a reward for obedience. While some might well laugh, I behave especially well before an important Michigan football game, as if wins or losses depend upon my current spirituality rating. Although humorous, superstition blinds me to grace. In the Reformed tradition, as much as we emphasize salvation by grace, I depend upon my actions to make me right with God. Millions of Christians, especially Catholics, live every day with the confining belief that their acts determine the extent of God's favor. It is folly to presume to project the purposes for God's intervention or inaction.

At more cogent moments, I am grateful that Jesus' death means that I will not get that which I have earned. Periods of suffering are ironically those times when life is most fair. Whether I receive two or three or ten lucky breaks from heaven, God offers not one stroke of good fortune as spiritual salary. Instead, my faith grows only when I recognize Christ's grace to be sufficient for me and forsake attempts to earn further blessing. Since God refuses the role of cosmic Genie of the Lamp, blessings serve as gifts to further service rather than good-behavior bonuses. Neither does hardship constitute some foretaste of hell. I praise God for rejecting meritocracy, because I know I can never measure up to his standards. My heart rests more easily when I live solely within the sufficiency of God's grace.

Luke 13:18–21

> Then Jesus asked, "What is the kingdom of God like? What shall I compare it to? It is like a mustard seed, which a man took and planted in his garden. It grew and became a tree, and the birds of the air perched in its branches." Again he asked, "What shall I compare the kingdom of God to? It is like yeast that a woman took and mixed into a large amount of flour until it worked all through the dough." {NIV}

Do we ever ask God do great things in Jesus' name? Do we humbly suggest to the Lord that he display his remarkable grace through us? Do we remind Jesus that an immense miracle would be appropriate? I regularly make grandiose requests because I can find no reason why I should settle for less from God. In my nightly prayers, I have laid at God's feet the salvation of Sudan, India, China, Costa Rica, Germany, and many other countries. Perhaps even more audacious than intercession for countries, I have pled with God for history's lost souls, even the likes of Fidel Castro and Gene Simmons. If Cruella De Vil were not a fictional character, I would take a shot. I test Jesus' assertion that even a small dose of faith will accomplish feats as magnificent as throwing Herod's manmade mountain, so modestly named the Herodion, into the sea.

Jesus encourages us to indulge our spiritual dreams. He reminds us that no matter how small we feel, great things come in trifling packages. Mathematics shows us that a small number (in our case a small kingdom act) multiplied by infinity (in our case eternity) achieves a momentous result. The smallest ripple of an eternal wave moves an infinite amount of water. If God chooses me to do a little here and there, my contribution remains remarkable. Kingdom work is qualitative rather than quantitative. God so values his children that any good done for anyone is infinitely significant. My seemingly unimportant contribution may be the mustard seed that expands into a great tree. The history books do not celebrate Martin Luther's mother, but we know that she shaped the great reformer, her small work being the mustard seed from which grew the second millennium's greatest tree. We are never to limit God's creativity or eagerness to do great things with our gifts.

So when my contribution appears to be nominal, disillusionment cannot squelch my trust in God. Since he has carefully gifted me, he will not waste my efforts. God transforms my prayers into intercession of immeasurable qualitative greatness. He turns my hopes, my prayers, my gifts, and my works, even if rumored to be pedestrian, into a splendid contribution. I can rest assured that he will hold up his end of the bargain. Jesus has sacrificed his own soul to satisfy his boundless love for creation, so will he not grant my request to participate in the redemption of creation? Neither the product of sinful pride nor wicked arrogance, a bold approach to God's throne epitomizes obedience, loves others, and empowers me to fulfill the wildest ambitions of a servant's heart.

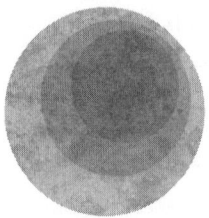

Luke 14:1–6

One Sabbath day Jesus was in the home of a leader of the Pharisees. The people were watching him closely, because there was a man there whose arms and legs were swollen. Jesus asked the Pharisees and experts in religious law, "Well, is it permitted in the law to heal people on the Sabbath day, or not?" When they refused to answer, Jesus touched the sick man and healed him and sent him away. Then he turned to them and asked, "Which of you doesn't work on the Sabbath? If your son or your cow falls into a pit, don't you proceed at once to get him out?" Again they had no answer. {NLT}

Perhaps a frustrated playwright, Luke treats us to some first-century theater as he unveils his masterpiece, *When Hypocrites Attack VII*, a harbinger of unfortunate things to come from the Fox Broadcasting Network. Similar to *When Hypocrites Attack I–VI*, this half-hour drama again pits Pharisees against Jesus regarding the merits of doing God's work on the Sabbath. Luke's Gospel, like the rest of Scripture, repeats teachings and themes. Through multiple literary and personal styles, the Bible creates an intricate mosaic with a straightforward message, simple enough in its emotional invitation for any sinner to embrace.

I thank God that kingdom membership extends beyond the spiritually gifted. It is axiomatic that a God who spent so much time with lepers and sinners would make his kingdom accessible to simple folk. I can sum up the gospel in three sentences, without losing anything but the intricacy: All men have sinned, thereby forfeiting their natural relationship with God. Christ has paid for our sin on the cross, and he offers us salvation by grace. Christians live in faith and gratitude, seeking to reflect Christ in love, obedience, and service.

As a teenager, God blessed my heart at a Christian youth convention as kids shared with two thousand peers the details of their hardships and God's solutions. Some were so emotionally invested in their testimony that they could hardly muster the words to explain their thoughts. For an evening, we all stepped back from the intricacies of theology to meditate upon the truth that *God loves people*.

While I want to better understand the delicate theological

tapestry, I best understand biblical truth in light of the motto of the game *Othello*: "A minute to learn, a lifetime to master." The understanding of Scripture more closely reflects racquetball than golf. While a beginner in goggles can quickly master a few basic rules and skills before spending years enjoyably running into walls, golf confounds the masses giving joy only to the dedicated, the experienced, and the wealthy. A trip in an airplane's first-class cabin will leave one wondering both how anyone can talk so much about the intricacies of his game and whether any golfer actually finds more joy than frustration in his beloved pastime. Scripture should not be so confounding.

I enjoy the complexity of God's providence and it feeds my faith. The grand eloquence of Augustine, Calvin, Aquinas, and Luther has revealed great mysteries of the kingdom. Yet, complexity cannot distract us from a simple gospel. The Bible neither repudiates knowledge nor permits book learning to numb us to the Holy Spirit's touch. As I reread Scripture, if tempted to skim over familiar waters, maybe I should examine whether the message has sunk into my heart.

Luke 14:7–14

Jesus saw how the guests had tried to take the best seats. So he told them: "When you are invited to a wedding feast, don't sit in the best place. Someone more important may have been invited. Then the one who invited you will come and say, 'Give your place to this other guest!' You will be embarrassed and will have to sit in the worst place. When you are invited to be a guest, go and sit in the worst place. Then the one who invited you may come and say, 'My friend, take a better seat!' You will then be honored in front of all the other guests. If you put yourself above others, you will be put down. But if you humble yourself, you will be honored." Then Jesus said to the man who had invited him: "When you give a dinner or a banquet, don't invite your friends and family and relatives and rich neighbors. If you do, they will invite you in return, and you will be paid back. When you give a feast, invite the poor, the crippled, the lame, and the blind. They cannot pay you back. But God will bless you and reward you when his people rise from death." {CEV}

Our culture neither venerates humility nor tutors modest behavior. The Hollywood elite raise narcissism to an art form as stars parade by to hand out an endless supply of awards celebrating their own performances. They covet the Academy Award, which they give to each other, and the People's Choice Award, which the secret Ordinary People Club must hand out. Each star feigns disdain for the paparazzi while posing for photographs. Joan Rivers critiques the celebrities that meander down the red carpet, judging whether each luminary exudes style and glamour. *People Magazine* annually selects the world's fifty most beautiful people, who by some miracle of probability all live in New York or California. These magnificent fifty express surprise about the recognition. If Descartes had been an American, he would have said, "I love me, therefore I am."

Jesus insists upon true humility, not a cloak behind which the shrewd hide self-interest. We sin when we see obedience as a means to acquisition, when service becomes a race for the best seat at the big feast. By God's grace, my spiritual reward grows as others join God's kingdom. He will some day show me how each prayer, kind word, or loving act has assisted another's spiritual journey. God empowers me to lift others to greater kingdom success, an act that diminishes my comparative importance but increases my joy. My greatest spiritual treasure is the neighbor who met Jesus through me. King David tells me in Psalm 23 that my cup will overflow with spiritual excess. While treasure talk conjures up images of selfishness, Jesus says to be ambitious for the kingdom. So in all humility, I will with great energy gather for the kingdom as many people as I can reach, an audacious and unreasonable pile of spiritual loot.

Luke 15:1–2

> Tax collectors and other notorious sinners often came to listen to Jesus teach. This made the Pharisees and teachers of religious law complain that he was associating with such despicable people—even eating with them! {NLT}

My uncle died without a perceptible relationship with the Lord Jesus Christ. According to my father, my uncle gave up on the church and turned his back to the Lord as a young boy during the Great Depression. Undernourished and clothed in dilapidated rags, my uncle's Sunday School teacher scolded him for defacing the Lord's house with his unsuitable clothing. Decades did nothing to soften an impressionable child's resentment, and my uncle never again returned to the cold church building that substituted for a warm house of prayer.

We all arrive at the Lord's throne room clothed in tattered rags. Although wise souls slip in through the side door, we too often prefer the main gate, where photographers can properly shoot the poorly stitched "good works" that hang unflatteringly from our shoulders. We wave off compliments concerning the supposed fine workmanship of our deeds, which cling to us with the thinnest strands of faith that can pass as a belt or a button or a pin. In place of shame for our inability to perfectly keep God's law, we hope that bravado covers the muddy stains of sin that despoil even our Sunday best.

In addition to exaggerating our own stylishness, we join those who castigated Jesus for fraternizing with sinners as we lift our chins and crinkle our noses at those who struggle with immorality. Invoking an illusory caste distinction between sinner and saint, we turn our peacock tails toward the most prolific of visible offenders. I click my tongue at the spiritually unfashionable, and my pride begs me to evict those haggard in their piety. I forget how much I like to hang out with the sinners as I remind Jesus that those whom he loves are unworthy of my time and attention.

I cannot understand why I so naturally embrace something as intuitively evil as the prideful banishment of my neighbor. I shake my head at my neighbor's worn clothing as I push him to the netherworld of insignificance. Satan loves to convince Christians to substitute his pride for God's love. My uncle rejected Jesus because Christians would not set aside their vanity to embrace a misfit child. While Satan would have me believe that I appear as a prince rather than a beggar, I pray that God would instead exchange my rotting homemade garments for a "hand-me-down" washed by God himself in the blood of his only begotten Son.

Luke 15:3–10

Then Jesus told them this story: "If any of you has a hundred sheep, and one of them gets lost, what will you do? Won't you leave the ninety-nine in the field and go look for the lost sheep until you find it? And when you find it, you will be so glad that you will put it on your shoulder and carry it home. Then you will call in your friends and neighbors and say, 'Let's celebrate! I've found my lost sheep.'" Jesus said, "In the same way there is more happiness in heaven because of one sinner who turns to God than over ninety-nine good people who don't need to." Jesus told the people another story: "What will a woman do if she has ten silver coins and loses one of them? Won't she light a lamp, sweep the floor, and look carefully until she finds it? Then she will call in her friends and neighbors and say, 'Let's celebrate! I've found the coin I lost.'" Jesus said, "In the same way God's angels are happy when even one person turns to him." {CEV}

From earliest childhood, I have occupied comfy quarters in the Lord's sheepfold. Perhaps you can picture that room. My bed rests along one wall, near the carpet indentations where my parents' knees rest as they pray. The fragrance of their prayers lingers in the room. Also near my bed, a children's Bible lays open on my nightstand, relatively new because such gifts come often, yet somewhat worn because family members read me stories about the Lord. Across the room is a rocking chair that my parents use to hug me and remind me of the Lord's boundless love. Guarded by an army of stuffed animals, my room glows with the Lord's presence, a place where I rest my head without fear or discontent. It is a great blessing to grow up in the Lord's flock.

Although God has blessed me with a wonderful sheepfold, I am the quintessential lost sheep. My blessings fail to constrain me from being self-reliant and eager to discard God. I explore valleys, slip on rocks, fall into pits, drink bad water, and stumble into a myriad of sheep-like activities. Others may also slip out the gate at night, but God must consider me to be an especially problematic sheep or the Good Shepherd is very busy searching for the lost. I am the poster-sheep for divine patience, the beneficiary of every opportunity, but determined to wander off.

Despite my obstinacy, Jesus scrapes his knees on rocks and fights through thorns to search for me through the moonless night. He seeks not to acquire smarter sheep, but reclaims the stray that indulges in folly. He carries me home, only to see me walk away to again be found. Thank God that we lost sheep cannot match the relentless shepherd. In light of the angelic musical celebration over each salvaged sinner, more than one sore throat will accompany my arrival in heaven. In gratitude, I must make every effort to return to the sheep-pen by curfew. However, as one who frequently loses track of time, I am delighted that God will again come looking for me.

Luke 16:1–9

He also said to His disciples: "There was a certain rich man who had a steward, and an accusation was brought to him that this man was wasting his goods. So he called him and said to him, 'What is this I hear about you? Give an account of your stewardship, for you can no longer be steward.' Then the steward said within himself, 'What shall I do? For my master is taking the stewardship away from me. I cannot dig; I am ashamed to beg. I have resolved what to do, that when I am put out of the stewardship, they may receive me into their houses.' So he called every one of his master's debtors to him, and said to the first, 'How much do you owe my master?' And he said, 'A hundred

measures of oil.' So he said to him, 'Take your bill, and sit down quickly and write fifty.' Then he said to another, 'And how much do you owe?' So he said, 'A hundred measures of wheat.' And he said to him, 'Take your bill, and write eighty.' So the master commended the unjust steward because he had dealt shrewdly. For the sons of this world are more shrewd in their generation than the sons of light. And I say to you, make friends for yourselves by unrighteous mammon, that when you fail, they may receive you into an everlasting home."
{NKJV}

In law school, I dated a woman who loved to receive greeting cards. It mattered little whether a card commemorated Valentine's Day, a birthday, Christmas, or—even better—nothing at all. Since my idea of romance was Rocky Balboa screaming, "Aaaadwian," cards were nothing more to me than something to which I paid polite attention before opening the real gift. After months of work, my girlfriend had convinced me to buy cards for special occasions, even the periodic "just because you are you" day. Soon Hallmark's greatest hits no longer sufficed, and she requested handwritten thoughts on each card. One day, I found a card with an overstated, but plausible, little poem. When I could produce no handwritten harmony to accompany my store-bought sensibility, I begged God for romantic inspiration.

If only I had listened in English literature to the sonnets written by the great poets, Byron, Shelley, and Bon Jovi. Inspiration struck as I realized that I needed no advice from Don Juan; my friend Machiavelli would do just fine. With insight maybe from above, maybe from within, but probably from below, I purchased a second Hallmark gem. I copied the original poem onto the second card and threw away the incriminating evidence. My girlfriend later bubbled with joy as she read the poetic words that Mr. Hallmark had crafted and that I had copied. While I had heard that hell hath no fury like a woman scorned, I also knew there was nothing to fear when you care enough to steal the very best.

Jesus congratulates the shrewd manager for his foresight in unjustly transforming transient wealth into permanent friends. In my opinion, the lost beatitude must read, "Blessed are the deceptively clever for they shall not be caught." In light of such an easy path to cynicism, Paul has wisely excluded shrewdness from his list of spiritual gifts. Our sinful nature too easily tempts us to shift from cunning behavior to actions that ignore our biblical mandate to love our neighbors as ourselves. We can, however, still learn from the shrewd manager. Jesus admonishes us to use time and possessions to endear ourselves to God. Since neither earthly friends nor heavenly angels can intercede for me before God, Jesus remains the only friend whose favor I must court. Unlike other friends, namely wealth, power, and pleasure, Jesus alone can shelter and restore me. A shrewd manager, having already received his termination notice, whether two weeks or eighty years hence, wrestles away what Satan has stolen. The shrewd manager returns time, talent, and wealth to the master's service. A shrewd manager has limited time and gifts, but much to do.

Luke 16:10–15

Anyone who can be trusted in little matters can also be trusted in important matters. But anyone who is dishonest in little matters will be dishonest in important matters. If you cannot be trusted with this wicked wealth, who will trust you with true wealth? And if you cannot be trusted with what belongs to someone else, who will give you something that will be your own? You cannot be the slave of two masters. You will like one more than the other or be more loyal to one than to the other. You cannot serve God and money. The Pharisees really loved money. So when they heard what Jesus said, they made fun of him. But Jesus told them: "You are always making yourselves look good, but God sees what is in your heart. The things that most people think are important are worthless as far as God is concerned." {CEV}

Throughout school, my friends would engage in many an evening of Napoleonic conquest as our respective armies, mine preferably green, swept across continents mapped out in the board game Risk. We were discontent with the game as designed, so we created new maps and playing pieces to raise the level of intrigue. Notwithstanding our additions, the principles of Risk were unchanged. Each player conquered territory and built up armed strength, all the while looking to launch a masterstroke—a sweeping attack that would conquer a continent or eliminate a rival scheming genius. The tension increased as one wrong move would send my neighbor's hoards streaming over my borders like a plague of invading Mongols. Faces twisted in concentration, as each would-be conqueror planned the onslaught of his waiting forces.

While I hope for many evenings of spiritual conquest in my journey with God, my prayerful preparation lacks the devotion that I dedicated to my role as Risk general. I remember lying awake at night begging God for a wife. God must have questioned how I could ask to be entrusted with one of his precious daughters when I historically did not guard my thoughts against impurity. I ask God to supply me with resources and expand my talents, but I prove to be undisciplined in smaller tasks. A bit red faced, I press on, suggesting to God that if he blesses me monetarily, I will give much back to support the church. God must grieve over my devotion to money and wonder why he would make steward over his resources one who skimps on his tithe and falsifies other financial matters. Yet, I pray with a straight face that God will allow me to do great things for the kingdom.

I need to place the horse of spiritual preparation before the cart of spiritual blessing. I cannot ask God to spill his armies across the border, indifferent to waste and oblivious to menace. Should he carelessly authorize me to march out to war when I clumsily fritter away troops and pursue objectives not his own? I cannot suggest to God that I cannot hear him respond to my prayers because his biblical instruction keeps buzzing in my ears. While I have been a poor steward to date, thank God he chooses to work through imperfect instruments. The Holy Spirit will make me trustworthy in great matters should I, as servant, commit myself to concerns like purity, conscientiousness, and generosity. God will transform the most meager beating of my faithful heart into a thundering drum calling others to his peace. Whether or not he grants me what I request, I must make myself fit for any role that God chooses.

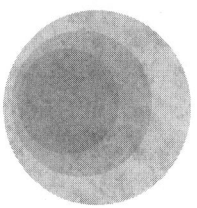

Luke 17:3–10

So be careful what you do. Correct any followers of mine who sin, and forgive the ones who say they are sorry. Even if one of them mistreats you seven times in one day and says, "I am sorry," you should still forgive that person. The apostles said to the Lord, "Make our faith stronger!" Jesus replied: "If you had faith no bigger than a tiny mustard seed, you could tell this mulberry tree to pull itself up, roots and all, and to plant itself in the ocean. And it would! If your servant comes in from plowing or from taking care of the sheep, would you say, 'Welcome! Come on in and have something to eat'? No, you wouldn't say that. You would say, 'Fix me something to eat. Get ready to serve me, so I can have my meal. Then later on you can eat and drink.'

> Servants don't deserve special thanks for doing what they are supposed to do. And that's how it should be with you. When you've done all you should, then say, 'We are merely servants, and we have simply done our duty.'" {CEV}

Most westerners consider religion to be synonymous with ethnicity or culture. We Americans breeze through our *Reader's Digest* religion survey, quickly confirming our skin color and hair texture before checking, Buddhism, Hinduism, Judaism, Islam, Catholicism, or Protestantism. Religion resembles eye color, something inherited from parents for no greater reason than that a grandparent handed down the same religious faith. For many, religion weaves itself through the tapestry of where we come from, but has little effect on where we are going. Cultural faith instead generates traditional carnivals and ethnic rituals such as Christmas, Ramadan, or Yom Kippur, rites that we observe much like drinking beer at Oktoberfest or eating sausage at the Polish Festival. Surely, faith means more than ethnic lineage.

Most Christians consider faith to be synonymous with mere *belief*. In *The Empire Strikes Back*, after Luke Skywalker fails to raise his battered X-wing fighter from the swamp, Yoda closes his eyes to concentrate upon "The Force," and the bog easily gives back its prize. In response, Luke exclaims, "I don't believe it," to which Yoda replies, "That is why you fail." Could such belief move a mountain? The answer is no. Many an hour I spent squeezing my eyes shut and puffing out my cheeks, straining in vain to levitate my dad's Ford Pinto off of the driveway. Surely, faith means more than meager conviction.

As envisioned by Jesus, faith calls us to action, even discomfort. God imposes upon his children an obligation, derived from duty rather than request, to labor in his fields. Once we complete one task, God assigns us another endeavor. Such obligation offends our democratic spirit, but will the gospel according to Rousseau save you from sin's grasp? While faith commandeers my effort instead of my vote, Jesus promises to transform the tiny seed of my contribution into a great tree of blessing to others. I must confess my fear because I see little return on God's investment. Even we spiritual weaklings cannot blame a poor performance on powerlessness. I will not treat the master's call as a measly request to heed at my convenience. Notwithstanding the roots of heritage and the comfort of belief, faith without works is dead.

Luke 17:11–19

As Jesus continued on toward Jerusalem, he reached the border between Galilee and Samaria. As he entered a village there, ten lepers stood at a distance, crying out, "Jesus, Master, have mercy on us!" He looked at them and said, "Go show yourselves to the priests." And as they went, their leprosy disappeared. One of them, when he saw that he was healed, came back to Jesus, shouting, "Praise God, I'm healed!" He fell face down on the ground at Jesus' feet, thanking him for what he had done. This man was a Samaritan. Jesus asked, "Didn't I heal ten men? Where are the other nine? Does only this foreigner return to give glory to God?" And Jesus said to the man, "Stand up and go. Your faith has made you well." {NLT}

We desperately want to earn our salvation. Whether by nature or by culture, we would rather bargain with God than accept charity from heaven. While God has promised grace to Abraham, I would still peddle my paltry deeds to God as payment for sin. My study Bible commentary reinforces this mistake. The commentary suggests that Jesus may have conferred eternal life, in addition to physical healing, upon the one grateful Samaritan. I squirm at the inference that the nine ungrateful lepers received no such dual gift. Should we surmise that the thankful man derived salvation from his gratitude? Salvation originates from the Redeemer's grace, not the redeemed's tasteful appreciation. Although gratitude for grace is appropriate, we face as great a temptation to earn salvation through thankfulness as by any other good work.

I smile because the unappreciative nine did not forfeit their blessing from Jesus or reacquire leprosy as a result of their thanklessness. Ingratitude does not disconnect us from God or displace Jesus' grace, which is by definition undeserved. No work, not even thankfulness, can replace Jesus as the way, the truth, and the life. Important as they are, good deeds cannot bridge the chasm that separates us from God. Nor can sins of omission, even ingratitude, separate us from peace with God, which Jesus has purchased for us at great cost. Personally, I would have it no other way.

While it cannot separate us from Christ, ingratitude is nevertheless tragic. The Samaritan, unlike the unappreciative nine, basks in the Lord. He praises God loudly and fully participates in the Lord's joy. Gratitude operates as a prism, breaking the light of blessing into all its radiant color, while ingratitude numbs believers to the splendor of their divine gift. The thankless nine do not forfeit access to God's throne room, but the Samaritan absorbs every spectacle, smells every aroma, and delights in every dulcet tone. The act of counting blessings does not multiply their number or increase my spiritual dragon's horde, but reveals the Father's generosity.

Luke 18:1–8

One day Jesus told his disciples a story to illustrate their need for constant prayer and to show them that they must never give up. "There was a judge in a certain city," he said, "who was a godless man with great contempt for everyone. A widow of that city came to him repeatedly, appealing for justice against someone who had harmed her. The judge ignored her for a while, but eventually she wore him out. 'I fear neither God nor man,' he said to himself, 'but this woman is driving me crazy. I'm going to see that she gets justice, because she is wearing me out with her constant requests!'" Then the Lord said, "Learn a lesson from this evil judge. Even he rendered a just decision in the end, so don't you think God will surely give justice to his chosen people who plead with him day and night? Will he keep putting them off? I tell you, he will grant justice to them quickly! But when I, the Son of Man, return, how many will I find who have faith?" {NLT}

My prayer life parallels the modern stereotype of a widow's influence upon her society. Television commercials paint today's widow as helpless—giddy about that Clapper gadget that replaces her inattentive relatives in lighting the reading lamp. Likewise, I pray with no expectation of divine attention. My appeals to God are dust in the wind, hanging briefly in the air, but then swiftly blowing away at the first gust of inconvenience. Prayerful diligence rarely enters my vocabulary, much less puts scabs on my knees. Rather, I am content with prayerful trinkets, essentially junk not worth the asking. Commercials also portray today's widow as lonely, convinced that her Chia Pet is truly a tasteful decoration with which to converse. Likewise, I pray with no expectation of a personal relationship with God. I chatter out the same stale petitions, never listening for an answer, never pausing to really talk to God. In light of my example, Jesus asks whether the Son of Man will find faith on the earth.

The widow in Luke faced a desperate task, appealing to a judge who neither feared God nor respected men—a judge who was uninterested in and unsympathetic to her plight. Despite her hopeless quest, she knocked relentlessly on his door. In the evening, the judge strained to sleep over her banging. In the morning, he awoke to her calls. In the afternoon, she stood in the pounding rain or the beating sun, waiting for and insisting upon an audience.

This widow shames me. My judge wants justice and exudes mercy. When I fail to appear at his doorstep, he looks for me on the streets, calling my name, inquiring whether there is anything I need. He invites me over. He answers promptly, even when it appears to be a long wait. He wants me to ask for much and to expect more. The Lord dotes like any parent, instructing and prompting, hoping that we will step out in faith. The widow challenges me to throw away my Clapper and shatter my Chia Pet, because rich spiritual gifts from the Holy Spirit's hand and a personal relationship with the Messianic King are there for the asking.

Luke 18:23–30

But when the man heard this, he became sad because he was very rich. Jesus watched him go and then said to his disciples, "How hard it is for rich people to get into the Kingdom of God! It is easier for a camel to go through the eye of a needle than for a rich person to enter the Kingdom of God!" Those who heard this said, "Then who in the world can be saved?" He replied, "What is impossible from a human perspective is possible with God." Peter said, "We have left our homes and followed you." "Yes," Jesus replied, "and I assure you, everyone who has given up house or wife or brothers or parents or children, for the sake of the Kingdom of God, will be repaid many times over in this life, as well as receiving eternal life in the world to come." {NLT}

While some seek acclaim for their hard work or achievement, I labored to become a master of lowered expectations. My older brother became "crown-victorian" of his class, earning a tepid nod of approval from my father who *expected* such levels of achievement from him. By way of contrast, my mother cheered wildly with relief as I meandered across the stage to collect my high school diploma. In my initial college gym class, I walked along slowly, staring in bewilderment, as my classmates blew by me in the twelve-minute test run. How were these people going to earn an A, in a class undoubtedly graded on improvement, if they challenged world records for distance running on the first day? My motto was "If you want something done, give it to a busy person," a philosophy that earned me a ton of free time. If my acquaintances expected little, then I could not disappoint.

Contrary to my *modus operandi*, Jesus tells the rich young ruler that God expects so much that a camel can squeeze through the eye of the needle (which was in the Jewish tradition a picture of a very small place) more easily than a rich man can enter God's kingdom. So much for my God of Lower Expectations—the accepting Grandfather that society elected to replace the Old Testament hardliner who destroyed cities, unleashed floods, and evicted garden variety tenants for picking apples and streaking in public. Thanks to Marlin Perkins, I know that a grown camel could never push its body through such a small hole. In the modern vernacular, Jesus might say that it is easier for my dog to remove the plastic from a compact disc than for a rich man to enter Heaven. Absent divine intervention, the rich clearly have no hope of entering heaven.

Who are the rich anyway? Jesus includes all who cling to worldly life. Worldly riches can be money, power, pleasure, or a host of other idols that grab the first fruits of my attention. We are all rich because we firmly entrench ourselves in this world and covet its illusory treasures. Just as the leopard cannot change his spots, so we cannot change our camel-like nature.

Recognizing my predicament, God graciously offers to push me through the eye of the needle. Although I gaze at temporal idols, God pushes and prods until he coerces or even forces me into his kingdom. Magnificent salvation, an undeniable miracle in light of our sinful blight, truly belongs to our God. Although American culture tells me to take charge of my future, I prefer God's path. I delegate my task to God with whatever words and sounds camels use. Since I cannot meet God's standard, I rejoice that what is impossible for us camels is miraculously attainable for and wondrously desirable to the Creator of camels.

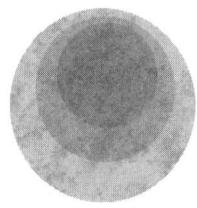

Luke 18:35–43

When Jesus was coming close to Jericho, a blind man sat begging beside the road. The man heard the crowd walking by and asked what was happening. Some people told him that Jesus from Nazareth was passing by. So the blind man shouted, "Jesus, Son of David, have pity on me!" The people who were going along with Jesus told the man to be quiet. But he shouted even louder, "Son of David, have pity on me!" Jesus stopped and told some people to bring the blind man over to him. When the blind man was getting near, Jesus asked, "What do you want me to do for you?" "Lord, I want to see!" he answered. Jesus replied, "Look and you will see! Your eyes are healed because of your faith." Right away the man could see, and he went with Jesus and started thanking God. When the crowds saw what happened, they praised God. {CEV}

Likely a beggar dependent upon the good will of his fellow citizens, the blind man probably rushed to the street, stumbling and bumbling about, calling out to Jesus. The locals tried to quiet him, but the blind man continued to embarrass his neighbors by raising a fuss. The further they pushed him from the traveling dignitary, the louder he shouted his request for mercy. This man scraped and clawed to achieve his one ambition, an audience with the master.

Like the blind man in the story, the spiritually and physically sick exert extraordinary effort to make their way to Jesus, demonstrating their acute sensitivity to God in times of need. Their "blindness" dominates their thoughts and causes them to cry out boldly and persistently for God's restoration. Oblivious to embarrassment they call out "Marco, Marco," searching for the answer "Polo" that will identify the savior. It is not surprising that such burdens would push people toward a savior. Those with greatest needs best suppress their pride.

While I sometimes denounce those who show heightened interest in God during times of need as fair-weather Christians, maybe God welcomes this behavior. Pain and infirmities remind people of their need for spiritual fortification. We know that Paul first clearly saw his God through eyes darkened by blindness. Is it not a great blessing if, in troubled times, the soul, which bears the very image of God, innately reaches for the Christ?

As God shapes his children for service, those who cry out to Christ in need most resemble him. My mother, who has spent her life working with emotionally challenged children, comments that those "afflicted" with Down Syndrome are among the most loving of people. Who better lives in the daily joy of the Lord, me or the handicapped person in my church? Over the years, I have approached God in both sin and suffering. I bring no worthy gift on these pilgrimages, and my pressing need for clemency or comfort clearly displays itself upon my arrival. Yet, the Lord always heals me, and always grants me a parting gift of greater compassion for others. I hope that my eyes are sufficiently blind to see that which drives me back to the Father.

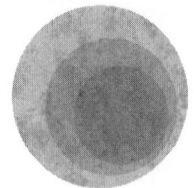

Luke 19:1–5

> Jesus entered Jericho and was passing through. A man was there by the name of Zacchaeus; he was a chief tax collector and was wealthy. He wanted to see who Jesus was, but being a short man he could not, because of the crowd. So he ran ahead and climbed a sycamore-fig tree to see him, since Jesus was coming that way. When Jesus reached the spot, he looked up and said to him, "Zacchaeus, come down immediately. I must stay at your house today." {NIV}

For all the platitudes that Christians apply to Jesus, etiquette and social grace do not fall among them. I imagine Zacchaeus scrambling in the branches, hurriedly toppling out of the tree to satisfy the demands of coerced hospitality. Jesus huffs, puffs, and blows the door down, leaving poor Zacchaeus to entertain this peculiar guest who had invited himself to dinner. Yet, Jesus' invasion of Zacchaeus' home is only the tip of this iceberg. Impervious to normal limits of social bravado, Jesus manipulates this man's life, showing no respect for Zacchaeus' autonomy. He instead discards Zacchaeus' old life in favor of one more to his liking. Jesus' transformation of Zacchaeus must have left many, including Zacchaeus himself, shaking their heads in wonder at the little tin man, the joyful owner of a newly refurbished heart.

I am a soft knocker, one who taps lightly on doors and hearts alike, careful not to be a bother. I tiptoe and tap, keeping my thoughts to myself, hoping that my presence will be wanted by others. Unfortunately, sometimes I display an equally tepid commitment to Christianity. Content to hide in the cheap seats, I avoid the sycamore tree that would make me visible to Jesus and subject to his request for dinner. I prefer to eat by myself.

But when Jesus does invite himself for dinner, (in secret, I am grateful that Jesus, not Zacchaeus, initiated their encounter), I rush to greet him as an honored guest as Zacchaeus would do, hustling to venerate him by washing the dirt off of his feet in keeping with the Jewish custom. Mary Magdalene leaves God's feet bathed in perfume, dripping with the tears of forgiven sin. The disciples describe God's feet nailed to Golgotha's cross in payment for lost sheep. Modern Christians imagine God's feet leaving footprints in the sand as he carries his precious child through life's hardships. Though I too often offer no such reverence, God nevertheless wedges his disrespected foot in the door of my heart, refusing to permit me to slam that door in his face. Martin Luther has written that our God is a mighty fortress. Notwithstanding Luther's wise words, perhaps our God is as much a battering ram as a fortress. When my Baptist friends ask when I gave my heart to Jesus, I respond that no such event ever occurred. Rather, the God who humbled Jericho's great walls has forced the door and invited himself in to take up residence. I expect that he will take my whole lifetime to clean up the splinters that once were the door which separated him from his prize.

Luke 19:6–10

Zacchaeus quickly climbed down and took Jesus to his house in great excitement and joy. But the crowds were displeased. "He has gone to be the guest of a notorious sinner," they grumbled. Meanwhile, Zacchaeus stood there and said to the Lord, "I will give half my wealth to the poor, Lord, and if I have overcharged people on their taxes, I will give them back four times as much!" Jesus responded, "Salvation has come to this home today, for this man has shown himself to be a son of Abraham. And I, the Son of Man, have come to seek and save those like him who are lost." {NLT}

Despite his current popularity in children's songs, the locals knew only Zacchaeus the Traitor and Zacchaeus the Thief. The

Jews reviled Zacchaeus the Tax Collector, perhaps even more than they despised Samaritans and lepers. Zacchaeus ranked below those whom God had apparently forsaken and ostensibly cursed. With reckless disregard for his person, Zacchaeus jostled with the crowd, hoisting himself into a sycamore tree. Zacchaeus needed a serviceable viewing perch, even if uncomfortably visible to the crowd, from which to observe the great teacher. When Jesus stopped to speak to him, Zacchaeus further incited the crowd by hosting Jesus at his home, a place desecrated by sinful collaboration with the Romans. In pursuit of Jesus, Zacchaeus took center stage among those who rightfully hated him.

While Zacchaeus has become the patron saint of short people, we would better emulate him as role model for the spiritually hungry. Nothing about Zacchaeus' appearance or deeds would naturally enshrine him in any hall of heroes. Is it startling that Michelangelo chose the splendid David over the diminutive Zacchaeus as the ideal of Renaissance man? A lengthier gaze, however, reveals a subtle truth. Although Jesus spoke first, Zacchaeus relentlessly pursued God, totally conforming himself to God's expectations. Would I not naturally respond to Jesus' challenge by asking forgiveness and then boldly stating I would no longer steal from my neighbors? Instead of my half-heartedness, Zacchaeus promises not only to stop thieving, but to restore significantly more than he had stolen. He is unyielding and generous in his newfound spiritual service. It is this Zacchaeustic spiritual enthusiasm rather than Napoleonic bluster that the minstrels should forever extol as the enduring characteristic of the vertically challenged.

Luke 20:9–19

He went on to tell the people this parable: "A man planted a vineyard, rented it to some farmers and went away for a long time. At harvest time he sent a servant to the tenants so they would give him some of the fruit of the vineyard. But the tenants beat him and sent him away empty-handed. He sent another servant, but that one also they beat and treated shamefully and sent away empty-handed. He sent still a third, and they wounded him and threw him out. Then the owner of the vineyard said, 'What shall I do? I will send my son, whom I love; perhaps they will respect him.' But when the tenants saw him, they talked the matter over. 'This is the heir,' they said, 'Let's kill him, and the inheritance will be ours.' So they threw him out of the vineyard and killed him. What then will the owner of the vineyard do to them? He will come and kill those tenants and give the vineyard to others." When the people heard this, they said, "May this never be!" Jesus looked directly at them and asked, "Then what is the meaning of that which is written: 'The stone the builders rejected has became the capstone'? Everyone who falls on that stone will be broken to pieces, but he on whom it falls will be crushed." The teachers of the law and the chief priests looked for a way to arrest him immediately, because they knew he had spoken this parable against them. But they were afraid of the people. {NIV}

I imagine watching God walk through a garden in the pale light of dusk. Satan makes an unwanted appearance, dancing in circles around the Father as the creator strolls through the trees. Finally, the Father says, "Let me tell you about my servant Job." Satan quickly interrupts, "Yeah, yeah, yeah, we have already been over that one. Let meeee tell youuuu about your other servant." Lucifer begins a long narrative of *my* adventures, an endless catalogue of my shortcomings.

"You have a tenant to whom you have given wealth, a man who lives free of illness and blessed by comfort. He is a vain, selfish, and useless man. You have sent servants to harvest fruit from his life. Have you heard the reports? He has rebelled against wisdom and humiliated friends standing for Jesus. He has constructed an obedient façade to scare off those who would instruct him and make him useful. You have sent more servants to harvest fruit from his life. Have you heard the reports? He has rejected Paul and ignored John the Baptist. In place of Paul's 'cultural baggage,' he prefers tolerance as more relevant to modern man. In place of John's submission, he chooses his own path. You have sent your son to pull him from the pit. Have you heard the reports? He has smashed the covenant tablets. He has with the crowd, cried, 'Crucify him! Crucify him!' He swings the hammer hard, driving the nails deep into Jesus' wrists at every opportunity. You have stripped everything from Job, and he honors your name. You have blessed this malcontent, and he shames your house."

The Father walks away, knowing that the master of lies has spoken nothing but truth. From a hill overlooking the garden, I wonder what manner of grace prevents the Lord from unleashing his rage. My heart explodes in fear as I realize, even in a moment of panicked prayer, that I will again beat the messenger and reject the olive branch. Fear overtakes me as I think that the Father's rightful vengeance, justice, and holiness necessitate that he remove any trace of me from creation. My hands tremble and my lips inaudibly repeat the words, "May your blood cover me Lord." In the distance, the master walks on, burning with fierce anger restrained only by greater grace, resolute beyond both this penitent's hopes and that worm's contemplation.

Luke 20:27–40

Then some Sadducees stepped forward—a group of Jews who say there is no resurrection after death. They posed this question: "Teacher, Moses gave us a law that if a man dies, leaving a wife but no children, his brother should marry the widow and have a child who will be the brother's heir. Well, there were seven brothers. The oldest married and then died without children. His brother married the widow, but he also died. Still no children. And so it went, one after the other, until each of the seven had married her and died, leaving no children. Finally, the woman died, too. So tell us, whose wife will she be in the resurrection? For all seven were married to her!" Jesus replied, "Marriage is for people here on earth. But that is not the way it will be in the age to come. For those worthy of being raised from the dead won't be married then. And they will never die again. In these respects they are like angels. They are children of God raised up to new life. But now, as to whether the dead will be raised—even Moses proved this when he wrote about the burning bush. Long after Abraham, Isaac, and Jacob had died, he referred to the Lord as 'the God of Abraham, the God of Isaac, and the God of Jacob.' So he is the God of the living, not the dead. They are all alive to him." "Well said, Teacher!" remarked some of the teachers of religious law who were standing there. And that ended their questions; no one dared to ask any more. {NLT}

These verses are my favorite New Testament text. Some rightfully cherish John 3:16, while others treasure Romans 8, and still others cling to the fruits of the Spirit. Yet, I vote for an argument about heavenly marriage. My love for these verses parallels the Pharisees' dearest belief that the God of Abraham, Isaac, and

Jacob reigns as God of the *living*. I grab hold of these verses because they declare that Jehovah, Lord of the universe, will raise my body up from the dust and restore my every dream.

The Sadducees rejected as fairytale the very idea of resurrection. They mocked Jesus and chided the Pharisees for propounding such an inane concept. Hardly disguising their snickers, they conjured up impractical questions for Jesus, trying to expose him to ridicule. Jesus refused to waiver and repudiated the secularism so beloved by the Sadducees. Jesus' words reminded believer and unbeliever alike that all Israel, both Jew and eventually Gentile, could claim the title "children of the resurrection." After the ensuing silence, a Pharisee replied, "Well said, Teacher." The formerly taunting Sadducees asked no further questions.

Resurrection alone offers a reason to love and a purpose to serve. Why should I love unless people are more than dust? Why should I serve unless my work survives the test of time? Only creation's renewal saves us from the obliteration of a contracting universe or the meaninglessness of a universe cooling into inactivity. We all sense this truth. Paul tells us that without resurrection, we should be pitied beyond all men, those of us who speak of hope, a word without meaning if death is the end of the line. With apologies to Disney for disproportionate disparagement, we cannot agree that Simba the Lion King will find true hope in a meaningless circle of life. We can still visit the Great Pyramids, huge monuments that ancient Egypt dedicated to misguided preparation for death. Against this backdrop, the resurrected Jesus affirms that God is God of the living. The hymn-writer correctly prophesies that "Death cannot hold its prey." When we read Luke, maybe we should not be so quick to skim over thirteen verses about who marries whom.

Luke 21:1–4

> And He looked up and saw the rich putting their gifts into the treasury, and He saw also a certain poor widow putting in two mites. So He said, "Truly I say to you that this poor widow has put in more than all; for all these out of their abundance have put in offerings for God, but she out of her poverty put in all the livelihood that she had." {NKJV}

Televangelists insist, of course in the egalitarian spirit, that every person, no matter how impoverished, can obtain great wealth by forwarding their last pennies for the construction of the Jesus World theme park. The Lord despises such health and wealth ministry. Americans would want Jesus to conclude his story by telling us that the poor widow triggered sirens and streamers as the temple's well-compensated ten-millionth customer. However, Jesus does not suggest that the woman found even an evening meal. There is no hint of a white knight or promise of a golden ticket in a lucky chocolate bar. We know instead that Joseph spent years in Pharaoh's jail, Moses tramped forty years in the desert without ever setting foot in the promised land, and that David fled from both his king and his son. The fruit of the spirit, the gift package that we receive from God when we embrace Jesus as Lord, does not include physical possessions or comfort or even a worldly souvenir.

We live at a time when we can fashionably talk a lot of spiritual trash. I enjoy listening to athletes thank God for styling them bigger, faster, and more gifted than their colleagues. We hear our cue and praise God, unfortunately loudly, for his excess "blessings," otherwise known as money. We bow our heads to cheap grace or, more accurately, easy service, convincing ourselves that we serve God when we sacrifice a second BMW or when we donate convenient time. We carefully avoid dropping anything of value into the passing plate.

God focuses upon my heart rather than my "voluminous" giving. While he entrusted all my gifts for kingdom service, the cosmic Creator prefers my soul to my donation. As father, he wants me to empty my needs into the coffer. He would have me lift my eyes from their steady gaze on the dusty path to take in the forest, hills, and lakes that surround me. The widow's two minas bring praise from Jesus and reflect a heart at peace with God, a reward worth more than bags of money or years of comfort. I have heard radio interviews with Jim Bakker, now serving God in Los Angeles' housing projects. The newly poor Jim Bakker sounds happier than the old Jim Bakker who rode in limousines procured by spiritual fraud and tax evasion. A wise man holds nothing back, but empties his pockets of every dime, talent, hope, sorrow, and prayer. While some would be uninterested, the Lord settles for nothing less than my two measly minas.

Luke 21:5–28

Some of his disciples were remarking about how the temple was adorned with beautiful stones and with gifts dedicated to God. But Jesus said, "As for what you see here, the time will come when not one stone will be left on another; every one of them will be thrown down." "Teacher," they asked, "when will these things happen? And what will be the sign that they are about to take place?" He replied: "Watch out that you are not deceived. For many will come in my name, claiming, 'I am he,' and, 'The time is near.' Do not follow them. When you hear of wars and revolutions, do not be frightened. These things must happen first, but the end will not come right away." Then he said to them: "Nation will rise against nation, and kingdom against kingdom. There will be great earthquakes, famines and pestilences in various places, and fearful events and great signs from heaven. "But before all this, they will lay hands on you and persecute you. They will deliver you to synagogues and prisons, and you will be brought before kings and governors, and all on account of my name. This will result in your being witnesses to them. But make up your mind not to worry beforehand how you will defend yourselves. For I will give you words and wisdom that none of your adversaries will be able to resist or contradict. You will be betrayed even by parents, brothers, relatives and friends, and they will put some of you to death. All men will hate you because of me. But not a hair of your head will perish. By standing firm you will gain life. "When you see Jerusalem being surrounded by armies, you will know that its desolation is near. Then let those who are in Judea flee to the mountains, let those in the city get out, and let those in the country not enter the city. For this is the time of punishment in fulfillment of all that has been written. How dreadful it will be in those days for pregnant women and nursing mothers! There will be great distress in the land and wrath against this people. They will fall by the sword and will be taken as prisoners to all the nations. Jerusalem will be trampled on by the Gentiles until the times of the Gentiles are fulfilled. "There will be signs in the sun, moon and stars. On the earth, nations will be in anguish and perplexity at the roaring and tossing of the sea. Men will faint from terror, apprehensive of what is coming on the world, for the heavenly bodies will be shaken. At the time they will see the Son of Man coming in a cloud with power and great glory. When these things begin to take place, stand up and lift up your heads, because your redemption is drawing near." {NIV}

A great mystery emerges from the destruction of Herod's temple and the other signs of the times regarding God's kingdom. While scholars debate whether I should mark apocalyptic events on my calendar, even John Calvin has avoided commenting upon the ambiguities of eschatology. Novels about eschatology are interesting, but I fear that such fiction gives instruction about the end times in a fashion similar to which Kirstie Alley and Patrick Swayze teach us our Civil War history in the made-for-TV miniseries *North and South*. We know who wins in the end, but everything in between is hyperbole at best and complete fabrication at worst. The end times are unknown in shape and form, a great but mysterious Rosh Hashanah, a magnificent but inexplicable messianic coronation, a spectacular but unexplained historical culmination.

Although I am young, the Lord has not left one stone upon another. I have lost loved ones to death, friends to betrayal, and dreams to the world's rigors. Hardly a year passes during which Satan fails to attempt to chisel away at my spiritual foundation. I at times walk without hope, familiar with despair, and acquainted with apathy. Why does God allow Satan his day? Why must God use this life to test, and temper me, if he means in the next life to redeem and restore me? The winds of apocalyptic mystery swirl about me, drown out the answers to my questions, and raise dust in my eyes.

Yet, the master course of stone remains in place, an immovable object that Martin Luther has described as a mighty fortress and that John Rippon has pictured as a firm foundation. The prince of darkness cannot surprise or supplant the Christ. False prophets and tribulation cannot loosen either the king's gentle grip on my heart or his stranglehold on my sin. I know that Satan will obliterate every earthly temple. I know that the four horsemen of the apocalypse will leave me standing alone, lifeless and desolate. Though I stand in the valley of the shadow of death, though the world burns in the background, though I have nothing, I have Jesus.

Luke 22:14–22

When the hour came, Jesus and his apostles reclined at the table. And he said to them, "I have eagerly desired to eat this Passover with you before I suffer. For I tell you, I will not eat it again until it finds fulfillment in the kingdom of God." After taking the cup, he gave thanks and said, "Take this and divide it among you. For I tell you I will not drink again of the fruit of the vine until the kingdom of God comes." And he took bread, gave thanks and broke it, and gave it to them, saying, "This is my body given for you; do this in remembrance of me." In the same way, after the supper he took the cup, saying, "This cup is the new covenant in my blood, which is poured out for you. But the hand of him who is going to betray me is with mine on the table. The Son of Man will go as it has been decreed, but woe to that man who betrays him." {NIV}

Have you ever heard the infectious and irrepressible laugh of a fledgling Christian? Spiritual enthusiasm wiggles behind a new believer's smile like a wet frog in a child's hands. A person cannot restrain the inherent desire, described by Pascal as a God-shaped vacuum, to know the Lord. God also wants intimate friendship, pursuing us even upon pain of death. The Christian revolution derives from one God, twelve students, and a series of small seminars on the hillsides abutting the Sea of Galilee. It interests me that Jesus eagerly anticipated rejoining his disciples after the Resurrection. Familiarity with Jesus enhances life with broad-brush strokes of color.

As God's image bearer, I naturally enjoy the company and well wishes of friends. While at work, I anticipate the lunch hour with its conversation and interaction. The weekends offer entertainment, but I better enjoy every activity when shared with another. My mother spends endless hours after Sunday services gabbing with her friends about matters both serious and trivial. At night, I remember the selfless acts of friends, the shared laughter, the unfortunate escapades, every means by which one Christian affirms the incalculable value of another.

Yet, friendships lack substance and stamina unless rooted in communion with the Lord. A godless friendship shimmers like a specter on a staircase, a haunting reminder of what once was, or what could be, but what is not. The devil creates shallow human interaction, relational plagiarism, to fill the void. Although a church without Jesus offers only futility and mediocre music, we have in our city a so-called church where one picks out beliefs like a new set of clothes, selected and tailored to one's preferences. I cannot believe that some rouse themselves from bed to trudge down to a church at which the Ten Commandments are no more authoritative than Christopher Robin's Ten Stay Safe Rules. Neither can I interest myself in an orthodox but Christ-less "church" that serves as a networking opportunity, a forum for self-congratulatory entertainment, or a launching pad for fortune-cookie psychology.

Thank God that the ultimate friend grips my heart. Whether we wander due to foolishness or rebellion, we find comfort because even Judas Iscariot ate the Lord's Supper at Jesus' left hand. Anecdotes abound to the effect that no person at death's door regrets time spent with God or family that could have been better invested in work or toys. He who finishes with the most toys wins? How can I better spend my time than in my Lord's company? In contrast to Kierkegaard's erroneous conclusion that Christianity expresses itself introspectively, the spirit-filled life explodes out from the salvation centrifuge, first to intimacy with God and then to selfless love for others. This relationship with the divine—the very purpose for our creation—is ours for the taking.

Luke 22:23–30

Then they began to question among themselves, which of them it was who would do this thing. Now there was also a dispute among them, as to which of them should be considered the greatest. And He said to them, "The kings of the Gentiles exercise lordship over them, and those who exercise authority over them are called 'benefactors.' But not so among you; on the contrary, he who is greatest among you, let him be as the younger, and he who governs as he who serves. For who is greater, he who sits at the table, or he who serves? Is it not he who sits at the table? Yet I am among you as the One who serves. But you are those who have continued with Me in My trials. And I bestow upon you a kingdom, just as My Father bestowed one upon Me, that you may eat and drink at My table in My kingdom, and sit on thrones judging the twelve tribes of Israel." {NKJV}

Years ago, I observed the strange afterglow of the funerals of Princess Diana of Wales and Mother Theresa of Calcutta. After Princess Diana died, yet hours before the passing of Mother Theresa, Michael Douglas, hardly the fount of wisdom, asked a rhetorical question: What would happen when a figure like Mother Theresa died? He was referring to the lavish funeral arrangements for Princess Diana. Several hours later and halfway around the world, Mother Theresa went home to be with her Lord. The results were predictable. Uninterested in Mother Theresa's faith, the world hailed them both as heroes for their mutual humanitarian instincts. I managed to catch just a little bit of Mother Theresa's funeral procession one night on C-SPAN. However, I watched the entirety of Princess Diana's funeral, having my choice of three major networks and limitless cable options. With the hubbub over the Princess, the withered old servant of the untouchables passed away comparatively unnoticed.

Who is great in the world's eyes? The Princess is great in the world's eyes because she drew attention to the sad state of our human condition. The Princess is great to the world because she was beautiful and glamorous and found love, notwithstanding broken marriage vows and the devastating impact of divorce. The Princess is "England's Rose" because she was a guiding light to others, she herself guided by a belief in reincarnation and a psychic advisor. By way of contrast, Mother Theresa, who accepted celebrity only as the price of serving as an example, fades quietly away, the power of her witness undermined by a stream of humanitarian rhetoric. I wonder who God thinks is great.

I believe Mother Theresa to be great, because she became worn and withered in service to God's prized untouchable children of India. Mother Theresa was great because she drew attention to the breadth of Jesus' mercy and God's tender heart. Mother Theresa's greatness lies in her pursuit of joy, righteousness, and truth rather than comfort and earthly happiness. I believe Mother Theresa to be great because she rejected worldly distraction in order to function as a window to the Father. Not even all of the trappings of a thousand years of English Christendom can change the fact the Princess Diana is a hero only in the world's eyes. Nor can all of the squalor and idolatry of Calcutta change the fact that Mother Theresa is a hero in the eyes of God.

Luke 22:39–46

Jesus went out to the Mount of Olives, as he often did, and his disciples went with him. When they got there, he told them, "Pray that you won't be tested." Jesus walked on a little way before he knelt down and prayed, "Father, if you will, please don't make me suffer by having me drink from this cup. But do what you want, and not what I want." Then an angel from heaven came to help him. Jesus was in great pain and prayed so sincerely that his sweat fell to the ground like drops of blood. Jesus got up from praying and went over to his disciples. They were asleep and worn out from being so sad. He said to them, "Why are you asleep? Wake up and pray that you won't be tested." {CEV}

The sun blazed brightly in the sky and the smell of spring carried on a light breeze, but the gloom of irreparable loss hung in the air. We walked through the funeral home, which was pleasantly furnished and politely manned, but served as a thin veneer covering something unnatural. Finding a place in line, we watched a conspicuously incomplete family greet those who had come to share their pain. An auto accident without apparent reason or any sense of appropriate timing had claimed the life of a son. People talked as they waited, not really caring about their conversations, but using mindless chatter to cover being ill at ease. Preferring somber contemplation, I concentrated upon hearing the Lord's whisperings at a moment when he strips away life's fallacies and distractions. While the Holy Spirit conferred upon the family an extra measure of peace, I could muster neither momentous answers about God's plans nor meaningful assurances. I could only share tears before walking away, muttering at God and knowing that the ramifications of incurable loss would settle in.

While some Christians worry that suffering is evidence of a lack of faith, Jesus teaches us to discard such worries. We empathize with a Christ whose trembling hands hold the cupful of sin and whose bowed head drips with blood as he begs his Father for another way. In light of our Lord's anguish, can we condemn our neighbors by attributing their affliction to faithlessness? Can we rub our Lord's tears of suffering between our fingers and still expect the mourning and personal regret from our own burdens to simply dissolve in Jesus' triumph over death? Neither our glorious future nor even an unshakable faith can place us beyond the reach of sorrow. Just like the sleepy prayers of the disciples, a friend's fellowship cannot remove the cross from the shoulders that bear its great burden. But through it all, the Father listens attentively as the psalmist sings out in sorrow, he watches intently as Jesus weeps in the night, and he grips the believer's suffering hand while misery lashes out in a final grasp at vengeance as grace extinguishes the last gasp of sin.

Luke 22:54–62

Having arrested Him, they led Him and brought Him into the high priest's house. But Peter followed at a distance. Now when they had kindled a fire in the midst of the courtyard and sat down together, Peter sat among them. And a certain servant girl, seeing him as he sat by the fire, looked intently at him and said, "This man was also with Him." But he denied Him, saying, "Woman, I do not know Him." And after a little while another saw him and said, "You also are of them." But Peter said, "Man, I am not!" Then after about an hour had passed, another confidently affirmed, saying, "Surely this fellow also was with Him, for he is a Galilean." But Peter said, "Man, I do not know what you are saying!" Immediately, while he was still speaking, the rooster crowed. And the Lord turned and looked at Peter. Then Peter remembered the word of the Lord, how He had said to him, "Before the rooster crows, you will deny Me three times." So Peter went out and wept bitterly. {NKJV}

As the morning light pours through my window, I spring out of bed eager to greet the crisp fall air that accompanies the arrival of Happinessgiving day. Although lacking Frosty the Snowman's joviality or the Easter Bunny's general fuzziness, the Happinessgiving turkey claims iconic status in American culture. The turkey symbolizes our celebration of excess as we wonder what manner of road kill John Madden has roasted into that eight-legged monstrosity. Some make an obligatory appearance at church after which we carefully inventory our bigger barns and count our many blessings one by one. When we eventually gather with our families, we stuff ourselves to the bursting point with every imaginable relish and dessert. America revels in surplus, listening wide-eyed as sportscasters offer trite phrases regarding prosperity and love of turkey.

Happinessgiving causes us to step back and survey our many reasons for pleasure rather than our deeper obligation to gratitude. While the Puritans thanked God for sufficient crops to survive the winter, the Fox Sports cameras worshipfully circle the eight-legged turkey, the stale symbol of our many gifts. We ignore the magnanimous Giver in order to glory in the "blessings" that surround us. We congratulate ourselves for receiving that which we deserve, and we wonder why other good people have seen such a run of bad luck. Although some might wrongfully accuse us of criticizing those thankful to God for earthly provision, we must reiterate that Happinessgiving celebrates nothing that does not succumb to the attack of moth or rust in the end. If I love my career, I will eventually lose my job or retire. If I cherish my family most, I know that even families spared the destruction of divorce will eventually surrender to death. If I treasure my stuff, college students will some day spill pizza grease on my precious furniture. True gratefulness, celebration of Thanksgiving rather than Happinessgiving, requires that God be the object of our affection. Otherwise, we condemn ourselves to stare lovingly at a vase without flowers, a reason to give thanks without a God to whom we can express our gratitude.

As strange as it might appear at first blush, the words "Woman, I do not know him," "Man, I am not," and "Man, I do not know what you are talking about," are the reason that I give thanks. Luke conscientiously reminds us of Peter's infamous denial, hammering home the truth that Jesus permanently claimed Peter for himself. Despite the oaths of betrayal, the passage tells us that Jesus looked at Peter, not that Jesus cut Peter off from the church. Scripture further teaches us that Peter did not wither away, but he became the rock upon which God built Christ's church, a servant who had done his task well. My permanent seat at the Lord's Table, despite my rebellion, is why I give thanks. Jesus has paid for my obstinacy and has secured my future. So on Thanksgiving, when popular culture bows down to the golden turkey in the Pilgrim suit, I will, with God helping me, take a moment to gratefully reflect upon the truth that "Woman, I don't know him" cannot break God's grip on my heart.

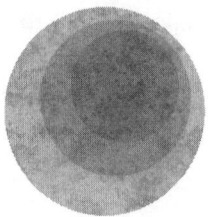

Luke 23:50–56

There was a man named Joseph, who was from Arimathea in Judea. Joseph was a good and honest man, and he was eager for God's kingdom to come. He was also a member of the council, but he did not agree with what they had decided. Joseph went to Pilate and asked for Jesus' body. He took the body down from the cross and wrapped it in fine cloth. Then he put it in a tomb that had been cut out of solid rock and had never been used. It was Friday, and the Sabbath was about to begin. The women who had come with Jesus from Galilee followed Joseph and watched how Jesus' body was placed in the tomb. Then they went to prepare some sweet-smelling spices for his burial. But on the Sabbath they rested, as the Law of Moses commands. {CEV}

Joseph of Arimathea, counsel member and follower of Jesus, walked the bleak Jerusalem streets leading to Pilate's palace on one final, respectful mission. Joseph wished to lay Jesus to rest with honor and in keeping with Jewish ceremonial law. Because his hopes and dreams hung from a cross, Joseph probably gave in to depression, acting more out of habit than hope. As he walked up to his dead Jesus and looked him in the face, little did he expect that God had planned a radical change for Joseph of Arimathea.

I love surprises, such as the unexpected resurrection of Jesus that awaited Joseph of Arimathea. To my family's chagrin, I hesitate to hand out Christmas lists for fear of ruining the surprise. While my sister has a long rap sheet for searching the house for a Christmas preview, I enjoy ripping the paper off each mysterious package. I likewise carefully avoid discussing movies I have not watched, and God help you if you tell me the score of a game that I am taping on the VCR. I search for new vacation locations, wonderfully unsure as to what sites and activities await me. When it comes to anticipated events, I firmly believe that what I do not know will not hurt me.

As I am sure that Joseph will confirm, God's surprises far surpass even the best bombshells we can conjure up in our minds. God's unexpected acts, as small as a surprise blessing or as grand as resurrection, give us hope and peace. Our God also loves surprises, routinely displaying his amazing propensity to renew our souls during our darkest days. Hopelessness will find me, but a God who raised the spirits of Joseph of Arimathea from hell itself certainly has some delightfully unexpected tricks up his sleeve for me.

Luke 24:9–12

So they rushed back to tell his eleven disciples—and everyone else—what had happened. The women who went to the tomb were Mary Magdalene, Joanna, Mary the mother of James, and several others. They told the apostles what had happened, but the story sounded like nonsense, so they didn't believe it. However, Peter ran to the tomb to look. Stooping, he peered in and saw the empty linen wrappings; then he went home again, wondering what had happened. {NLT}

It is interesting that I read these verses days after my family buried my mother-in-law. God comforts us in our distress and he sympathizes with our plight. Jesus' story consoles only because it describes resurrection and eventual conquest over death. My father-in-law is currently putting together a memory book about my mother-in-law to keep her memory fresh in his mind, current in our conversation, and at the center of his hope. While his loss is tremendous, his hope is greater. Without resurrection, a memory book would be a waste of time. This is the pivotal point in his life. As a family, we cling to resurrection because nothing else means anything to us.

The memory book is really not about memories. Although it contains pictures, narratives, and other memorabilia, history offers little comfort. Rather, the book provides a glimpse of the future. This book is a travel guide rather than a memoir, a prophecy rather than a biography. We can laugh and cry about the past only because we anticipate the future. We can anticipate the future only because Peter found a pile of loose grave clothes. Right now, we understand the futility of life without resurrection. Just as my week centered upon my mother-in-law's funeral, resurrection must drive my every thought and action. Only then can a memory book function not as a painful reminder of what was lost, but as a hopeful preview of what is to come.

Luke 24:13–32

Now that same day two of them were going to a village called Emmaus, about seven miles from Jerusalem. They were talking with each other about everything that had happened. As they talked and discussed these things with each other, Jesus himself came up and walked along with them; but they were kept from recognizing him. He asked them, "What are you discussing together as you walk along?" They stood still, their faces downcast. One of them, named Cleopas, asked him, "Are you only a visitor to Jerusalem and do not know the things that have happened there in these days?" "What things?" he asked. "About Jesus of Nazareth," they replied. "He was a prophet, powerful in word and deed before God and all the people. The chief priests and our rulers handed him over to be sentenced to death, and they crucified him; but we had hoped that he was the one who was going to redeem Israel. And what is more, it is the third day since all this took place. In addition, some of our women amazed us. They went to the tomb early this morning but didn't find his body. They came and told us that they had seen a vision of angels, who said he was alive. Then some of our companions went to the tomb and found it just as the women had said, but him they did not see." He said to them, "How foolish you are, and how slow of heart to believe all that the prophets have spoken! Did not the Christ have to suffer these things and then enter his glory?" And beginning with Moses and all the Prophets, he explained to them what was said in all the Scriptures concerning himself. As they approached the village to which they were going, Jesus acted as if he were going farther. But they urged him strongly, "Stay with us, for it is nearly evening; the day is almost over." So he went in to stay with them. When he was at the table with them, he took bread, gave thanks, broke it and began to give it to them. Then their eyes were opened and they recognized him, and he disappeared from their sight. They asked each other, "Were not our hearts burning within us while he talked with us on the road and opened the Scriptures to us?" {NIV}

One week ago, my family spent the day and evening greeting our community of fellow mourners. Over one thousand came that day, standing in line for two to three hours to extend a sympathetic and loving hand. My father-in-law personally greeted every last one of them, an exhausting but absolutely necessary task. One at a time, each gave a hug, a kind word, and a tear. Each expressed deep sorrow concerning the tragic loss of a beloved wife and an exceptional mother. My own dad reopened his own wounds as he shared with my brother-in-law how he too had lost his mother at age fifteen. Although precipitated by death and drenched in sorrow, this day belonged to the Lord. An army of marching Christians picked up the overwhelming cross of a needy family to suffer under its weight, and to lay it in its final resting place upon the back of a bloodied but risen Savior.

In this Luke passage, two friends walked together in melancholy, discussing the week's events and sharing their broken dreams. Jesus in no way discouraged this communion nor changed the context of their afternoon journey. Rather, Jesus shared in their lengthy discussion, eventually revealing his true identity, not in a flash of smoke and light but through everyday camaraderie. Even after disclosing his identity, Jesus' relationship with these now enthusiastic disciples did not qualitatively change. The two friends also remained much the same as they returned to share their joy with the remaining disciples. In community, not solitude, two Christians interacted with God and related to each other. No wonder that Saint Paul later described the collective church as a single living organism. On a cheerless afternoon, my family all walked the road to Emmaus with a church community making sure we did not stumble on the way, just as it was meant to be.

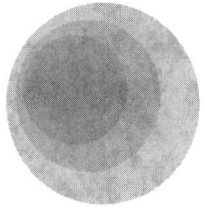

Luke 24:50–53

> When he had led them out to the vicinity of Bethany, he lifted up his hands and blessed them. While he was blessing them, he left them and was taken up into heaven. Then they worshiped him and returned to Jerusalem with great joy. And they stayed continually at the temple, praising God. {NIV}

At this time, the book of Luke comes to a close. Necessarily, my reflection on life in light of the good doctor's words also reaches its end. So as Jesus bid farewell to the disciples, I must say goodbye. Although nobody will ever confuse my best wishes for a blessing from the Lord, I sincerely hope that my hopes, reflections, struggles, and joys have helped you walk with Jesus through Luke. Likewise, though I by my own means cannot provide you with a meaningful blessing, I send you with prayers and the measure of the Lord's authority which Jesus grants to any Christian who prays for your welfare.

I also note that an atmosphere of joy surrounded Jesus' departure. This happiness, unusual in farewell, could only stem from the disciples' full knowledge that their physical separation from Jesus did not represent the end of their relationship but only an incomplete and temporary parting. Because Jesus is fully God, and because Jesus wields God's power by right of heredity and sacrificial deed, I know that my departure from you is similarly temporary, similarly incomplete, and similarly delightful.

Since you have read my literary meandering, it means that somebody has graciously decided to publish my words. I would be thrilled to meet with you again through some later work of ours, or perhaps some work of yours. However, should this little book extend only a short reach and should it prove to be primarily of assistance to me in my walk with God, I know that my relationship with you has not yet neared its full richness. Nonetheless, this little project has been the source of great joy to me, and I hope that it has been at least of a little assistance to you. So until we meet again in one way or another, we can leave you only the promise of our prayers. Somehow, that seems to be enough.